PRAISE FOR *QUIET THE RAGE*

"Intense, personal and vulnerable. This is a life lesson, generously shared, that might strike a chord and change a life."
–SETH GODIN, author of *Linchpin* and *The Icarus Deception*

"R.W. Burke shares his wisdom and insights about how to manage conflict well in *Quiet the Rage*. Read this book and prepare for a peaceful life!"
–MARSHALL GOLDSMITH, international best-selling author or editor of 35 books including *What Got You Here Won't Get You There* and *Triggers*

"What an honest, vulnerable, incredible journey! Burke's writing style is clear, concise, and bam—to the point! I will need to read this book more than once."
–LINDA GUTHRIE, Coach, Consumer Experience Movement, Ford Motor Company

"I have worked a lot on my anger; however, the info in this book is like discovering the missing link. Now, I have a much better understanding of why I get spun up in certain situations. I have a much better toolkit for dealing with my anger or avoiding it altogether."
–PHIL KLEIN, Facilitator, Maritz Performance Improvement, General Motors Standards For Excellence

"Great read! This book will change your life."
–BOB ESPOSITO, Dealer Principal, General Manager, Yankee Automotive Group

"This book is for everyone . . . especially someone like me who struggles with anxiety. It offers a way to take control back instead of feeling tossed by the waves."

–JENNIFER ROBERTS, Sales Manager, Genesee Valley Ford

"This book has forever changed the way I view interactions with people, both professionally and personally."

–JASON STANDLEY, Business Development Center Manager, Rowe Auburn/Rowe Westbrook

"The world needs more people who know how to manage conflict. Much of what is wrong in our society today could be changed if everyone understood how their anger is triggered. To adapt a quote from the cartoon character Pogo, 'I have met the enemy and it is me.' Everyone, even those who do not have a concern about rage, need to read this book."

–LINDA MITCHELL, author of *Choose Change . . . Before Change Chooses You! Thirteen Weeks To the Life You'll Love!*

QUIET THE RAGE

QUIET
THE
RAGE

How Learning to Manage

Conflict Will Change Your Life

(and the World)

R.W. BURKE, MBA, CPC

CERTIFIED PROFESSIONAL COACH

SPARKPRESS

Published by SparkPress, a BookSparks imprint,
A division of SparkPoint Studio, LLC
Tempe, Arizona, USA, 85281
www.gosparkpress.com

Published 2017
Printed in the United States of America
ISBN: 978-1-943006-41-0 (pbk)
ISBN: 978-1-943006-40-3 (e-bk)

Library of Congress Control Number: 2017945605

Interior design by Tabitha Lahr

To my wife, who has repeatedly, and continues to save my life.
I'm sorry for all the years that I couldn't have been more.

CONTENTS

FOREWORD

John Kuzava
Global Director I Engagement Strategies
Xperience Communications, LLC.

QUIET THE RAGE–
How Learning to Manage
Conflict Will Change Your Life
(and the World)

Richard Burke has written a magnificent collection of stories and insights all of which, in one way or another, flank and lead us through the tricky path known as transformation.

Reading through these carefully considered chapters of insight, introspection, and occasionally even humility, I have been reminded of various stories of transformation taught or shared with me over the years.

Although few of us think of this . . . the word story of course means just what it says . . . to store things. Long before management, consulting, and coaching books were written—in fact, before anything was actually *written*—stories were created to hold and *store* information that was needed to guide us through the complicated project called life.

Such stories are still with us today, having survived the centuries through oral storytelling; with a long history of generation after generation sharing, learning, and remembering their contents in order to safeguard and protect these precious insights and, in general, hold the ground for and share them with the next generation. This is why they are often considered children's stories.

In the opening chapters of this book, Richard shares some puzzlement regarding an assignment he accepted a few years back that would label him 'coach,' a role which essentially would give him access to the 'stories' of many individuals as well as the larger story-constellation of their organizations.

The word 'coach' of course has an interesting history and comes from the Middle French *coche*, the German *kotsche*, and the Hungarian *kocsi*—"(carriage) of Kocs," the village where it was first made—all are essentially words for carriage. And while we use the word today more often for 'preparing people', in a more poetic sense carriage is also accurate because a good coach provides something of a support underneath the people they work with. And that is certainly part of the mission of this book – to work in structured and perhaps invisible ways to add support underneath us in order to carry us forward and even through the various predicaments life serves up.

The focus of this book, though, is transformation.

There is something almost magical in that idea, let alone experience.

In becoming a coach, it is inevitable that one will find themselves excavating their own life, remembering and untangling stories that remain with us, anchored by great extremes of feeling, only to eventually find—hidden and lost amongst a lifetime of these twisting narratives—the gifts, talents, and resources we need to make sense of our journey.

I am reminded of a very old story from antiquity called "The Spirit in the Bottle." In this very old European story, we find the son of a woodcutter wandering the forest who discovers, lost and buried deep at the grassy roots of an old oak tree, a glass bottle with a voice inside calling, "Let me out!"

Uncorking the bottle releases a gigantic spirit who, instead of gratefully rewarding the boy, announces that it has been trapped so long that it is enraged and will now strangle him.

Being clever, the boy tricks the spirit back into the bottle and then they renegotiate the terms of its release.

Eventually the spirit is again released. This time, it rewards the boy with the gift of a cloth that, when rubbed on one side, turns things to silver and, when rubbed by the other side, heals wounds and illness.

We are familiar of course with this spirit by its commonly referred to name—Genie.

Genie is a very old North African word and the origin of our English word for genius.

Everyone has a genius trapped within them who grows more tired and angry over the years of being 'corked.' It isn't just people with IQs of 160 and above.

In a healthy life, we would have been told the right stories early on and would've been advised to be on the lookout for the genius and, more importantly, the gifts that the genius carries—such as transforming worthless things into value and also being able to heal those around us.

But few of us were actually told those stories when we needed to hear them while developing in childhood. So the genie within us waits well into adulthood, until it eventually finds its way out in a rage. By then, it has become gigantic—another way of saying 'too big to handle.'

If there is a role for a coach in this world, it is to help us find our trapped genius and to nimbly and cleverly help us get it under control, become productive, and to even reward us with the gifts it has been waiting all this time to give to the world. This is essentially the story Richard Burke has unpacked and broken down into well organized and understandable pieces we can recognize, understand, and apply in order to bring our best self forward for the good of the world.

PREFACE

Denise Burke

Many readers of my husband's book, *Quiet The Rage*, praise it for its raw honesty and how it uniquely describes and synthesizes the steps of managing conflict. I have a far more personal reaction to the penned words, however. Every line within this book represents the good, the bad, and the ugly of my husband's life; a life that I have spent living with him for the past thirty years. His words clearly detail the horror that unmanaged conflict caused for him, and for me in turn. As painful as some of this book was and *is* to read, it has become an essential part of my own path for personal conflict management. As someone once said: "the best apology is changed behavior." That's all I ever wanted.

REFLECTION:
THE SOURCE OF CONFLICT

"If you wanna make the world a better place—
Take a look at yourself and make that change."
—Michael Jackson, Man in the Mirror

There was a time in my life when I felt like I was in one endless argument, either with someone that worked for me, someone I worked for, a customer, or my wife at the end of a fourteen-hour day. I was doing a thankless job and living a thankless life. At its worst, I couldn't keep a job, and my wife admitted that she and my son were afraid of me because I was so explosive. Then one day, an opportunity that would change everything found me. In what could be characterized as serendipity—or in a more profound sense, some sort of divine intervention, perhaps a cosmic reordering—the circumstances that I needed to experience, at exactly the time I needed to experience them, presented themselves to me.

Since that pivotal moment, over the course of the last several years, my ability to interact with others has increased tenfold. I've been able to essentially eliminate conflict from my life—the conflict that was so terribly destructive for so many years—simply by synthesizing disparate information sources into one stepwise approach. It is exactly that approach which I believe led to me healing myself. I now have peace in my day, peace in my work, and peace in my life. My work is now purposeful; it is incredibly rewarding and fulfilling, and I feel blessed to be able to do well by doing good.

What's changed? I have learned to successfully manage conflict. The most beautiful, liberating, and empowering part of all is that anyone can do this. Managing conflict is a learnable skill. It's not rocket science; it's an almost unbelievably simple process—simple, but not easy.

Managing conflict begins by learning about one's and others' personal values. All human behavior is a function of those personal values. Conflict exists when someone feels like one of their personal values has been offended, or when someone feels like another is imposing their personal values upon them. Certain situations will be prone to offending those personal values, and in order to manage those "hot" situations, one must first identify them. When one encounters a situation that offends their personal values, it creates emotion. Emotion is the energy or fuel to drive *action*. In the case of conflict, it drives an emotional *reaction*.

The emotion exists because we are faced with someone else's behavior that challenges our world-view, our steadfast belief, that things are as we believe them to be . . . and only as we believe them to be. The emotion also exists because we are faced with someone's else's behavior that challenges the very idea of who we are or believe ourselves to be. We tend to interpret that behavior as being intentional: intentionally offensive. In our world, we expect people to behave in a certain manner, in keeping with the framework—the boundaries and the permissibilities—that we believe exists.

When another's behavior is not in keeping with our expectations of that behavior, we want to change it . . . sometimes forcefully. The emotion that results must then be *suppressed* or *expressed*. When suppressed, we withdraw, we stop communicating, and we feel helpless and powerless. When expressed, we lash out, we become angry and aggressive, argumentative and combative. One's emotional reactions create winners and losers. We are not our best selves, nor do we produce the best outcomes, when we are emotionally reactive. The challenge, then, is to see another's behavior for what it is: simply them honoring their values. Their behavior is about *them*; our reactions to their behavior, however, are about *us*. Those simple recognitions are the keys to interrupting an emotional reaction and creating the space necessary to transform the adverse emotional reaction into a beneficial response. This results in flipping entire interactions from negative to positive.

One painful thing (of many) I had to learn was that we sometimes create the behavior in others that we don't want. I was certainly guilty of that. The most painful, though, was that *I was the source of the conflict in my life*. When I stopped blaming myself and others, when I could take ownership of how I was contributing to the circumstances, when I heightened my self-awareness and developed other-awareness, when I stopped being the source of the conflict— *all of the conflict melted away*.

The moment I learned that *I* was responsible for creating all of the conflict in my own life was mind-bending and heart-stopping. It's also the exact instant that everything changed. I didn't know it then, but I spent most of my life contributing to, and participating in, a "Super Wicked Problem." A Super Wicked Problem exists when those who want to solve the problem are also causing it. So, the "aha!" moment for me was realizing that the conflict I was living through in life was of my own creation. Rather than looking around at others, I should have been looking at myself . . . in the mirror.

As we work through the process together, we'll dive more deeply into each of five steps. The **Realize** chapter focuses on identifying our personal values and our value-driven behavior. Assessing values is the first step in learning to manage conflict. The **Recurrence** chapter focuses on identifying situations that are prone to offend our personal values. Identifying those situations is the second step in learning how to manage conflict. It's important to be able to identify our "hot" situations in order to effectively to manage them. The **Reaction** chapter focuses on identifying our default mode of reaction. Understanding our reactionary style is the third step in learning how to manage conflict. Recognizing how we tend to react is necessary when wanting to take responsibility for one's behavior.

The **Rampage** chapter focuses on me and what drove my emotional reactions over the years. I explain how conflict pervaded my life, how self-survival mode quickly turned into self-destruct mode, and how a strength too strong became an epic weakness. The **Refrain** chapter focuses on techniques to interrupt the emotional reaction. Interrupting the emotional reaction is the fourth step in learning how to manage conflict. Within the interruption itself, there are two levels of abilities. One is reached by virtue of brute force; that is, learning to physically restrain the reaction caused by the emotion that exists. The other is reached when the emotion itself is no longer present, achieved by eliminating the perceived intentionality associated with the professed offensive behavior. There are some physical techniques, such as taking a breath, counting to ten, taking a walk, etc. But ultimately, your brain must interrupt the emotional reaction by recognizing the connection between others' values and the behavior that results.

The **Response** chapter focuses on transforming negative emotional reactions into positive responses. Transforming emotional reactions into responses is the fifth (and final) step in learning how to manage conflict. It involves flipping that negative interaction into a positive one, still allowing us to win, but no longer at others' expense. The **Resolve** chapter focuses on the entire stepwise process broadly applied, start to finish, with hope for a more peaceful future.

The **Readiness** chapter focuses on present-day precursors—the dynamics and circumstances that invited the change in me. The **Rage** chapter focuses on the catalysts; the events that shaped me, my worldview, my defensive orientation, and continuous strife. I spend the time to tell my story, because in the work that I do, people that struggle with conflict most say to me: "You just described my life." In a way, hearing my story helps them better understand their own. As such, it creates a bond, a kinship, between us, which couldn't exist if we hadn't shared histories. The **Reality** chapter focuses on my old view of the world, as flawed as it was. That perception informed my behavior. Like me, people hold themselves back, personally and professionally, based on their ability to get along with others. There were jobs I didn't get, and jobs that I got and lost, because I simply could not get along with others.

The **Reason** chapter offers a possible explanation for one's extraordinary sensitivity, and the seemingly perpetual struggle with conflict. When one's existence is at risk repeatedly, it is natural to revert to a self-survival mode. Too often though, long after the actual threats are removed, people continue to operate in that posture. It's what kept them safe, and where they are most comfortable. But as such, they unknowingly become stuck. Being stuck in self-survival mode is the surest way to incite never-ending conflict. The **Responsibility** chapter focuses on the idea of a *Super Wicked Problem: those that want to solve the problem, but are also causing it.* The only way to combat a Super Wicked Problem is to understand how one is participating in the problem, and then stopping that participation. The **Reckoning** chapter focuses on working through seemingly intractable problems. Some that stifle reason, disable rational arguments, and essentially paralyze every conceivable cognitive weapon that could be brought to bear against them, requiring wildly unsubstantiated assertions, or eliciting hyper-passionate emotions—my abandonment, for example. Conflict at its purest, ugliest, and rawest form, but worked through, nonetheless, by challenging and changing the nature of the problem; by challenging and changing my own perspective; by challenging and changing me.

Taken together, these are the things I learned that led to the elimination of conflict from my life. And only by *knowing* conflict, *living* it, and *being* it, can you truly value, promote, and enjoy peace. I share these things with you, with that same hope.

READINESS: THE ADVENT OF SELF-AWARENESS

"I am not afraid of storms for I am learning how to sail my ship."
—Louisa May Alcott

At forty-six, I hired on a project for a global automobile manu-facturer. By that time, I had spent twenty-five years working in and around the business. I had completed a bachelor's degree in accountancy, a master's of business administration degree with a concentration in finance, and was pursuing a certificate of advanced graduate studies in business intelligence. When I received my initial set of business cards, the title on them read *coach*. I still had cards from a project I worked a decade earlier, for a different global auto-mobile manufacturer. They preferred the title *facilitator*.

There are several titles that tend to be used interchangeably, such as consultant, coach, trainer, facilitator, and mentor. The terms are a little dubious, and the qualifications for someone to be dubbed as one or another are often that someone's veracity in claiming expertise in that area. Like law, the strength of the argument pre-vails, regardless of the underlying truth. The general contention among many who practice as one thing or the other is *they* feel they have the firsthand experience that qualifies them to perform the role, in spite of any real professional designation or actual training that would elevate their abilities in that particular area of practice. Many eschew the mere thought of pursuing any sort of credentialing; sometimes because of the cost or the time, but mostly for lack of humility. I admire that strength of character, but I didn't possess it. I felt like they could have titled me doctor, lawyer, engineer, dietician, exercise physiologist, or train conductor—it didn't make me one. Out of a sheer sense of inadequacy, driven by the insatiable need to *be more*, in combination with a sense of responsibility to those that I work with, I sought out a coach certification program. The program, I thought, would legitimize my day-to-day activities, provide a context to the work, and eliminate any challenge with respect to my work's efficacy. It was purely a defensive play.

After a fair amount of research (considering costs, geographic complications, time requirements, comparative rigor, and philosophical alignment), I selected the Institute for Professional Excellence in Coaching (iPEC), an affiliate of the International Coach Federation (ICF). In turn, iPEC had regional affiliates who were licensed and sanctioned to conduct training and certification of coaches on behalf of iPEC. Given its proximity, I selected New England Coaching, based in Marlborough, Massachusetts.

Start to finish, the program was scheduled out over ten months, culminating with an oral examination that couldn't be scheduled prior to thirty days past the completion of what we referred to as Mod 3 (Module 3). We were given up to a year after Mod 3 to turn in all of the written assignments, logs, and miscellaneous requirements necessary to graduate. It ended up taking me about eighteen months to satisfy those requirements, to earn the certified professional coach credential.

The program provided numerous challenges, not the least of which was adjusting to and juggling the workload. Some of the participants (about thirty in total) were out of work and seeking to re-train as Coaches, but many of us were already working full time. Mod 1, Mod 2, and Mod 3, as they came to be known, were scheduled on a Friday, Saturday, and Sunday, from 7:00 a.m. to 7:00 p.m., in the beginning, middle, and end of the ten-month curriculum. The Mods were scheduled roughly twelve weeks apart, which accommodated the Peer Coaching practice, woven-in, throughout the training.

Shortly after Mod 1, we received our initial coaching assignments. We were each assigned a Coachee; someone we would coach for an hour, on a weekly basis. We were also assigned a Coach; someone who would coach us for an hour a week. We were each assigned to a Peer Group, and would participate in a weekly conference call lasting an hour, to compare notes, support each other, challenge one another, and sometimes vent. In addition, each Tuesday night, we were required to attend a ninety-minute tele-class that dove into specific competencies required of coaches. All in all, it was four-and-half hours per week of practice and instruction for twelve weeks. After that period was over, the prospective coaches attended Mod 2, and the process of weekly coaching, being coached, and attending tele-classes repeated with newly assigned Coaches and Coachees.

In the second rotation, the Peer Groups became more specific with respect to their focus, and became Peer Special Interest Groups. We were able to elect among topics such as Life Coaching, Business Coaching, Relationship Coaching, Professional Coaching, Transition Coaching, Health & Wellness Coaching, Corporate and Executive Coaching, and so forth. Our peers, who were formerly classmates in the Mods, were now spread out around the country, unified by their choice of a particular Special Interest. The only additional layer of complexity was accommodating schedules, geography, and time differences.

Beyond attending the Mods and completing the four-and-a-half hour weekly routine for twenty-four weeks, we were required to complete a number of eWorkbooks on topics including "Intention Setting," "My Coaching Philosophy," and "Life Review," all designed to help expand our self-awareness. In addition, we were required to coach actual paying clients, and we were each assigned to a Mentor Coach, who would spend a total of three hours, broken into six thirty-minute intervals, evaluating our coaching ability.

For me, the greatest challenge in coaching was learning to ask questions, rather than providing answers. I had spent much of my life running businesses, solving problems, and establishing my value based in my ability to analyze situations, identify performance gaps, prescribe solutions, and then push people to execute on those ideas. My self-worth was solely based on my ability to do just that. I learned that that wasn't coaching, though. In fact, it was exactly the opposite of coaching.

Coaching as a profession believes that whatever someone is struggling with, whatever problem they are facing, whatever is limiting them in life, the solution to that struggle lies within that person. No solution proposed by the Coach will be nearly as personally satisfying and fitting as the solution proposed by the Coachee for themselves. The Coach's role is to move the Coachee forward—from the present to the future—moving them to action, attaching them to purpose, by virtue of asking powerful questions. Asking powerful questions is an art unto itself. And while it may sound easy, it is not. Especially when many of us had spent our lives asking closed-ended

THE ADVENT OF SELF-AWARENESS

questions to gain information so that we were able to form solutions. Habits remain, and breaking those habits is incredibly tough.

Consulting is about the consultant. It's about their experience, their solutions, their agenda, and they are the "fixers." As a former fixer myself, I measured my effectiveness based on my ability to fix. The focus on "how" to do something better, faster, differently, cheaper, more effectively, etc. Coaching is about the Coachee. It's about what they think, their ideas, their solutions, and only them. They don't want to be "fixed" —that implies something is wrong with them, that there is some deficiency in them. Fixing someone, then, is something we do *to them*. Coaching heals, and Coachee's *heal themselves*. The focus is on "want" to, rather than "how" to. As a former consultant, I learned the hard way—no amount of someone's knowing how to do something matters, until that someone wants to do that something.

So, coaching begins, continues, and ends, with powerful questions:

- "What would *you* like to focus on today?"
- "What would *you* like today's session to accomplish?"
- "How would *you* like to spend our time today?"

By answering, the Coachee provides the guidance, paving the way forward for the Coach and themselves.

- "I'm curious, why is that meaningful?"
- "How does that have meaning for you?"

Again, the Coachee will provide the answer.

- "What does success look like?"
- "How will you know when you've reached your goal?"
- "How will you celebrate that success?"
- "How would it feel if you were able to accomplish that?"

The Coachee will continue to move themselves forward, by envisioning something in their lives that they would like to be different. They will explain why that has meaning for them. They will paint the Coach a picture of the finish line. They will describe their feelings in vivid detail, imagining they have already achieved that success. They will become empowered and confident in their ability to positively impact the things in their lives that they are most dissatisfied with. The Coach follows with:

- "How committed are you to achieving those things in your life?"
- "On a scale of one to ten—with one being: "It sounds really hard, and I'm not sure I can do it" and ten being: "Get out of my way, I'm ready to move a mountain"—where are you?"

Again, the Coachee will provide the guidance. If the Coach is convinced that the Coachee is sufficiently committed, they may proceed to ask:

- "What's the first step that you could see yourself taking to achieve your goal?"

If the Coach doubts the Coachee's commitment, they might ask:

- "You said on a commitment scale of one to ten that you were about a five."
- "What could you imagine doing that might raise that number to a six or a seven?"

The Coachee will lay out their plan, either to raise their commitment or outline the first step toward success. The Coach might seek to bolster their confidence by asking:

- "What's a time in your past where you faced a similar circumstance that you were able to successfully navigate?"
- "What are some things that you learned from that experience that you might be able to apply here?"

The Coach will bring accountability by asking:

- "When would you like to have that done by?" and,
- "How do you prefer to be held accountable?"

Those simple questions remind the Coachee that the Coach will soon ask them:

- "When we last met, you said you wanted to: _____ by: _____ /_____ /_____ , were you able to achieve that?"

The Coach will search for how best to support the Coachee by asking:

- "How can I better support you in your effort?"
- "If that doesn't work, what else could you do?"
- "What's the worst that could happen?"

These questions, taken in total, result in a Coachee choosing something to positively impact in their lives, and then laying out a plan—start to finish—complete with first step actions, that are time-bound, that provide for contingencies, and explore the downsides. Not bad for what is often thirty or forty minutes in length. The key to the conversation is the forward progress, the solution oriented focus, and what iPEC refers to as raising the Coachee's energy.

QUIET THE RAGE

iPEC was founded by Bruce D. Schneider, author of *Energy Leadership; Transforming Your Workplace and Your Life from the Core.* iPEC teaches something called "Core Energy Coaching." The premise of Core Energy Coaching is that a person's thoughts and emotions manifest themselves in their physical bodies, and are expressed as "energetic levels." In iPEC terms, each level (think frequencies) has an energetic quality. The levels are described in a chart that iPEC refers to as an "Energetic Self-Perception Chart." **Level One**, for example, is **Victim** energy. Victim energy is characterized by neediness, lack of faith (in humanity, in the common good), lack of self-awareness, weak ego, *Apathy*, and *Lethargy*. Reluctance to rise up to defend oneself. The idea that the world is happening to them, and they are powerless to do anything about it. **Level Two** is **Conflict**—the focus of this book. Conflict is also marked by neediness, lack of faith and self-awareness, and weak ego, but diverges with respect to one's propensity to defend oneself. Conflict's hallmarks are *Anger* and *Defiance*. **Level Three** is **Responsibility**. If thinking in terms of positive and negative, Level Three—Responsibility—would be the first positive level. Level Three is characterized by *Forgiveness* and *Cooperation*. Self-awareness exists, faith is restored, and the ego is strong. Rather than neediness, Level Three celebrates having, not needing. **Level Four** is **Concern**. Concern's traits are *Compassion* and *Service*. **Level Five** is **Reconciliation**. Reconciliation's attributes are *Peace* and *Acceptance*. **Level Six** is **Synthesis**. Synthesis's characteristics are *Joy* and *Wisdom*. Synthesis divorces itself from ego and focuses on being, not having or needing. **Level Seven** is **Non-judgment**. Non-judgment's qualities are *Absolute Passion* and *Creation*.

As Coaches certified in Core Energy Coaching, we practice moving people through these energetic levels by understanding their current energetic state, and then asking powerful questions to raise their energy.

30

When I showed up to that first Mod 1 weekend, I was anxious to learn how to fix *others*. I wanted to get trained in the discipline, so that I was better qualified to do my job. As soon as the training started, though, it was clear that the focus wasn't on others. The focus was on *ourselves. Whoa!! Wait a minute!!* I thought. *I'm not here to examine my childhood, to expose old wounds, to bare deep feelings, to be . . . weak, or worse . . .* vulnerable.

Had I known in advance the path the training was to take, I probably wouldn't have done it. It was incredibly painful. But as I was to learn, change is a function of increased self-awareness and increased awareness of others. What a shock it was to find out, after forty-six years, I had neither.

RAGE: BORNE OF CONFLICT, BECOMING CONFLICT

"Sometimes they do somethin' to you Tommy.
They hurt you—and you get mad—
and then you get mean—and they hurt you again—
and you get meaner, and meaner—
till you ain't no boy or no man anymore,
but just a walkin' chunk of mean-mad.
Did they hurt you like that Tommy?"
—*The Grapes of Wrath* by John Steinbeck

Borne of Conflict

I was born in Bloomington, Indiana, in February, 1965. My mother met and married my father while he was in the Navy, stationed at the Naval Air Station Quonset Point, Rhode Island, in 1963. They subsequently relocated to my father's hometown shortly before I was born. My father's family was pretty well-to-do. The family business was lime quarries, cement factories, and the oil business—one of the family's holdings later became part of what is now Exxon Mobil. My father was raised in a thirty-two-room house, which was staffed with a small cadre of domestic workers. His father (my grandfather) died in the late 1950s of a persistent illness, so my grandmother headed the household. My father's uncles were all accomplished: a judge, a doctor, a stockbroker, and a Pulitzer Prize-winning journalist. Prior to passing, my grandfather was studying to become a doctor. My father's grandmother had graduated from Indiana University in 1905, uncommon in those days. His mother (my grandmother) graduated from IU and went on to complete a graduate degree at New York University prior to the Depression. Formal education was a way of life for my father's family, fully expected, not optional. Years later, the family homestead was gifted to IU, to become the site of IU's Kelley School of Business.

My mother attended college, but didn't finish, which I'm sure was a source of consternation for my father's family. She was the daughter of a factory worker. Her father worked in a soap factory in West Warwick, Rhode Island. Her mother, when working, worked in the cafeteria at a local college. Unsurprisingly, I've heard stories of my mother being scolded by my father's mother for fraternizing with the "hired help."

The Vietnam War was underway, and little did I know, a more personal war was in the offing as well. My parents separated by the time I was a year old. I was transplanted from Indiana to Rhode Island by my mother, who sought the refuge of her family and faith. My father didn't follow us to Rhode Island, and didn't cooperate with the divorce proceedings. As a consequence, they weren't officially divorced until the early 1970s. My mother suffered from a mental illness and was unable to care for me much of her life, but especially when I was young. I spent most of my early years with foster families and relatives, who (mostly) did their best to care for me. While I believe they meant well, it was clear that I was burdensome to them, and without getting into details that no longer matter, it wasn't a safe environment. It quickly became obvious that if there were two people on the planet that had no business having a child together, it was my mother and my father.

Because of being so young, it took several years until I realized the conspicuous absence of my father. Of course, I had a father, just not one present in my life. Not only was he not present, he did nothing to support my mother, which by extension, did nothing to support me. Regardless of what went wrong in their relationship, in as far as I was concerned, I had been abandoned. The ugly reality of being unwanted gave birth to my rage and my conflict.

Many people might have felt victimized by the circumstance. I suppose at some point, I must have felt that way too, though it was too long ago (or too painful) for me to remember. What I do remember, though, was being angry. Violent, explosive anger (rage) was my primary defense; it protected me, it kept me safe. As early as kindergarten, my temper got me into trouble.

Upon returning to Rhode Island, my mother tried to figure out how to get by on her own. Of course she had some support from family and friends, but not the kind that would relieve any of the crushing pressure that came along with being a "not-yet-divorced" single woman in the late 1960s. That status was viewed with disdain and dismay—"poor choices" was whispered. She did whatever it took to survive, including accepting assistance from anyone willing to oblige. As I was bouncing around from location to location, we would periodically be reunited. During one of those times, she had gotten me a winter coat. It was a fur coat. I had no idea where it came from; it could have been a hand-me-down from a friend or relative, it could have come from Goodwill, the church, I had no idea . . . and didn't care. She said that the football hero, Joe Namath, wore a fur coat, and when she saw it, it reminded her of that. I can remember proudly wearing that fur coat to school. That coat though, became a constant source of ridicule at school, kids being kids—in a less politically correct world—asserted that I was wearing a girl's coat. I remember aggressively defending my coat's honor. It was just a coat of course, but it was also symbolic of our plight. It was also another reminder that the effort, along with my sense of self, wasn't good enough. That painful reality always sparked the rage, and the rage led to endless confrontation. Inevitably, after being a chronic behavioral problem, I was suspended for fighting one day, and I'm pretty sure they asked my grandmother not to bring me back.

That period was incredibly tough for my mother as a woman, divorced, attempting to work, mentally ill, and with a child. I remember one night, I was probably four or five when we were living in someone's empty in-law apartment, she gave me a sip of what I thought was chocolate milk. She stepped away for a moment, and I didn't like the taste, so I poured it out in the sink. When she returned, she asked me where the drink was. I told her I didn't like it and had poured it out. She immediately broke down, sobbing at the kitchen table. I didn't know what I had done then. She never told me. But I know now—we had no food. I had just poured her only meal of the day down the drain.

My mother was remarried when it was time for me to attend the first grade. My new stepfather was divorced and had three kids of his own. My mother must have been searching for the exact opposite of her first husband when she found and married my stepfather. Over time, it became obvious that my stepfather and I were also polar opposites in every way. It would be a spectacular understatement to say that he and I got off on the wrong foot . . . more like the wrong leg, the wrong torso, the wrong body. I can remember being at my grandmother's house for dinner, just before they got married. It was me, my mother, my grandmother, my grandfather, and my stepfather-to-be. I must have dropped some food or a piece of silverware on the floor accidentally. My stepfather-to-be told me to pick it up. I told him that I wasn't going to pick it up, because I wasn't a maid. My grandmother intervened, picking up whatever I had dropped, relieving some of the tension and demonstrating her willingness to keep the peace. Once we had returned home, as I was getting ready for bed, my stepfather-to-be visited me with belt in hand, prepared with a lecture about the inappropriateness of my behavior. He then gave me an introduction to corporal punishment.

Forty-five or so years later, I now better understand the dynamic. Our value structure was simply different. My behavior offended some value of his. Maybe discipline, respect, compliance, deference, or humbleness. In turn, I was offended by the imposition of his values, on me. As such, I acted out . . . so did he. I created exactly the behavior in him that I didn't want, as he did in me. And now recognizing another point, that the rage in me became self-perpetuating; realizing I was unwanted by my "real" father for what I *was,* and unwanted by my stepfather-to-be, for what I *wasn't.*

I can remember being asked about the 1972 presidential election and the Vietnam War. My mother wanted to know who I would vote for (if I could) and why, and I responded that I would support Richard Nixon, because he promised to end the war. My step-father was incensed by that notion. He was a union electrician and supported the Democratic nominee George McGovern. While this is only one tiny example, it serves to illustrate the conflicting points of view that defined our relationship. As I got older, we clashed about everything. I considered myself a Republican, he considered himself a Democrat. I was baptized Catholic; he was a Protestant. I valued education and aspired to using my head to make a living; he saw little value in formal education, and made a living with his hands. To drive that point home, I remember when I turned thirteen, he grabbed me by the ear (literally) and took me to a local restaurant to see the owner. He told the owner I needed a job. As circumstances would have it, the restaurant owner needed a busboy and a dishwasher, so he hired me. My stepfather told me it was time I paid my share, and said that I was to pay fifty dollars a week in board until I moved out. I can remember he would tell me over and over that these were the best years of my life.

By working, I learned that I was good at work. I learned that I was good at drinking alcohol then, too. Being able to pay my own way was my ticket to freedom. I worked as much as I could, and when school got in the way, I didn't go. In my junior year of high school, I skipped the entire month of March. I probably wouldn't have gone back, but the school called my mother looking for me. I spent the rest of the year in in-house suspension. My teachers did their best to convince me that I was wasting my potential, but they couldn't answer my simple question: "How is the stuff you're teaching me (conjugating verbs, Venn diagrams, and the periodic table) going to help me survive *today?*"

Having suffered the loss of a biological father, and not wanting to lose a mother, I seized every opportunity to compete with my stepfather for the attention of my mother. I can still remember one afternoon while we were living in a converted summer campsite. I was probably nine or ten. My stepfather was having one of his relatives over to visit. He wanted to be sure that they didn't miss the turn into the campground, so he decided to greet them at the entrance, about a mile and a half away. He, my mother, and I walked up the dirt road about halfway. With about another three quarters of a mile to go, he asked me to run the rest of the way, just to be sure his relatives didn't miss that turn. The plan was that we would all ride back together. As I was running to the entrance, a number of cars passed me, one of which carried his relatives. After they passed, I turned around and ran back to where we originally parted. They were gone. They left me there, *alone*. I can remember being incredibly upset by my mother leaving me behind and choosing to go with him. When I got back to the house, my mother couldn't understand why I was so distraught. She figured I didn't want to tag along anyway. She didn't understand I felt abandoned by *her* as well. To make matters worse, I had competed with my stepfather and *lost*.

I once asked my mother why she got remarried. She said, "Because I wanted to have a life." I can better understand that now, but then I felt abandoned by my father and like baggage to my stepfather. Persona non grata, a quasi-bastard child, in a perilous lose/lose situation.

Given my mother's mental illness, she was periodically admitted for psychiatric care. One particular night, I can remember being awakened by a struggle at the front door, hearing my mother shouting that she didn't want to be taken away. Opening the door to my room, I remember my mother grasping both sides of the front doorway in an effort to thwart their attempts. I remember them not understanding my screaming and crying as I witnessed the unfolding events. They didn't seem to understand that I would be left living alone, again, with someone I considered a stranger. And they certainly had no idea that regardless of the circumstances, to me they were simply contributing to my neglect. There were many nights that I chose to sleep outside; sometimes in a neighbor's yard under a deck, in a shed, in a boat, or sometimes in my dog's doghouse (it was warmer) after having faked an invitation for a sleepover at a friend's house.

On my tenth birthday, after opening a gift from my mother, my stepfather put the wrapping paper in the wood stove. The paper caused a flash fire in the attic. Smelling smoke, knowing the house was on fire, he invoked his naval training. He had been trained that insulation would suffocate a fire. He used the hamper in the hallway as a makeshift ladder to get through the crawlspace into the attic. Despite his best efforts and the efforts of the local volunteer fire department, a good portion of the roof was gone. Later that evening, I remember sitting in the living room, looking at the stars through that hole in the roof. It wasn't ever said, but I got the sense that he blamed me—the gift wrapping on the gift my mother had given me sparked the blaze.

My stepfather wasn't immune to feelings, and I think the guilt he carried about his broken relationships with his own kids and the brutality of life wore on him. One evening, later that year, my mother asked me why my stepfather was crying. I said I had no idea. She explained that she had found him sitting on their bed, his hand wrapped in gauze, soaked in blood. She said that it wasn't safe to be around him, and that I should take her to one of my friends' houses so we could call for help. I remember walking through trails in the middle of the night, staying off the roads in case he came looking for us. I took her to a friend's house and did my best to explain the circumstances, not really understanding them myself. I just remember wondering where we were going to live.

I hated where we lived anyway. By then, I had lived in a half a dozen places in ten years. I was the youngest kid and the only only-child. The physical surroundings were fine, but the emotional space was rough. People toiled away making a living, scrimping and saving, living paycheck to paycheck—absent of hope, existing but not living. As the new kid, I was constantly picked on. But I always fought back. I didn't always win the fight, but whoever I was fighting knew they were in one.

I remember sometime before third grade—I must have been seven or eight, I was on house number five or so, new school, new neighborhood—I got into a fight with a neighborhood kid at the end of our driveway. There was a small crowd that gathered to support the other kid. We fought like kids our age. I must have gotten a bloody nose or something, and I went in the house to look for my mother. I remember my stepfather sending me back outside to finish the fight, which I did, to the bystanders' dismay. From then on, fighting was part of it. As I scan my memory of the past, I can't remember *not* fighting.

The kids in this newest neighborhood organized themselves in a *Lord of the Flies* sort of way, ruled by fear and force. The older kids were thuggish, more akin to young men than kids. They created all manner of havoc, destruction of property, breaking and entering, petty theft—what might be referred to as malicious mischief today. They enjoyed control and harassment. They would seize any opportunity to assert their will on the youngest of us. One day, we went somewhere by car. I needed a ride back, but they wouldn't let me in the car. They told me I'd have to ride on the hood if I wanted to get back home. So, I got on the hood. As you might imagine, a hell ride ensued . . . me holding on for dear life, and them enjoying the closest thing to bronco riding. Once we hit the dirt road, we did donuts, power-slides, panic stops—all with me on the hood. I try not to think about what could have happened, but focus on what did happen. I got home that day. That's all that mattered.

Most of us were unsupervised and left to our own devices. Whenever my mother wasn't around and I asked my stepfather about what I should do about something, he'd simply reply: "What would you do if I wasn't here?" So, I stopped asking, and I pretended he *wasn't* there.

The house across the street was sold, and a new family from Providence moved in. I got introduced to the youngest son in a deranged Darwinian kind-of-way. One of the other kids in the neighborhood said something about me being a "tough" kid. So, this new kid from Providence introduced himself by cold-cocking me in the head, saying that he was tough too. He was a tough kid. He had spent some time in a reform school, and his older brother and father had both done time in prison. I can't remember what led up to him shooting at me—we must have had an argument about something—but one day he grabbed a .22 caliber rifle and started shooting around my feet. Of course, I took off running, and the shots continued, all missing me. A few days later, the local paper referred to bullet holes being found in homes across the pond, about a quarter mile away.

Much the same way, as history making itself felt in the present, I finally realized that as I was getting older I was becoming a daily reminder of my biological father to my mother. So, as soon as I was old enough, I enlisted in the United States Army Infantry. Combat Arms. I fit right in. Fighting and surviving had become a way of life.

Becoming Conflict

I met my wife in 1988. I was working in the automobile business and fresh out of the United States Army Infantry. By that time, I had become a full-scale social combatant (a deadlier and more weaponized version of my former self) and a problem drinker. My mother and stepfather had asked me to move out of their house, because I was too uncontrollable and disruptive. That left me needing a place to live, so we decided to get married.

Most kids my age were scheming to become millionaires by

the age of thirty. My grand plan was to be dead by twenty-five. If I hadn't met my wife when I did, I probably would have been.

Shortly before I met my wife, I nearly died in a car accident. Alcohol, poor judgment, speed, and fatigue resulted in my car upside down—they estimated it flipped at 80 mph—on a lawn. I woke up in the hospital with severe pain in my right hand, explained by the fact that they believed it had gone through the windshield. The first responders said that based on the amount of blood in the car, they expected a fatality. After revisiting the accident scene upon being released from the hospital, I learned that the building the car ended up on was a Methodist church. *Fitting*, I thought. It was Easter Sunday.

I remember riding in the car with my mother at age five or six. She asked me what I wanted to do when I grew up. I told her I wanted to be an astronaut. She said, "Why would you want to be an astronaut? You could die." I remember telling her, "That's okay, Mommy, I'm not afraid of dying . . . everybody dies." Dying never frightened me. *Living* did.

My wife was from an Irish family, one of four children, and the only girl among three brothers. She was well-versed in conflict herself, as it was an everyday part of her existence. Her father had only one rule about who she could marry: Irish and Catholic. Fortunately, I was Irish, and I had been baptized Catholic. After my baptism, and following my mother's divorce, I was raised a Lutheran because my mother was no longer welcome in the Catholic Church . . . a slight that I still don't appreciate to this day.

I met my biological father for the first time in 1992, when I was twenty-seven years old. I learned that my paternal grandfather had died when my father was sixteen. So, in a certain sense, he had been abandoned as well. I also learned that I had the distinction of being the first of the family in a hundred years not to have attended college.

People ask me all the time: "What was it like, the first time you met?" They are always underwhelmed by my answer, as it is never what you want or imagine it to be. In truth, it was incredibly awkward. We tried for several years to forge a relationship, but it became obvious that my father didn't want to, or couldn't engage. Time and distance had taken its toll. It was painful to learn that I always wanted more than he could give. I can't fathom a parent not wanting to be part of their child's life. Realizing that this relationship wasn't to be again left me feeling unwanted.

In a remarkable irony, my son was born on Father's Day in 1997, after waiting eight years to have a child. The moment I first saw my son, I regretted every second, every minute, and every hour of that wasted time. His birth made my disconnection from my father all the more unfathomable. As a father myself now, I simply could not comprehend the thought of being absent from my son's life. My son's birth gave my father a third chance to be present in our lives. As I thought it might be too painful for him to revisit his relationship with me, I thought having a relationship with his grandson could be a fresh start for him and for us. It didn't happen. The most profoundly unforgivable disappointment was seeing my son unwanted by his grandfather.

I've come to think of these catalyzing events like stages in the launching of a rocket, each responsible for the continuous acceleration of the launch vehicle. As each stage burns off and falls away, the vehicle's overall mass decreases, allowing for more efficient propulsion. For me, it was the propulsion of rage; each heartbreak further enflaming it.

I won't say conflict ruined my life, but I will say conflict defined every part of it. My wife often referred to me as the "fuck-you guy," which pretty much summed up my desire and ability to get along with others. The part of me that wasn't good enough became ultra-sensitive to criticism, flying into blind rages whenever my performance was the least bit questioned, and further becoming hyper-competitive in an effort to continuously validate my worth. While very successful in business, my success tended to be at the expense of everyone around me. I've often been described as "the best manager we've ever had, but couldn't get along with anyone." It took many years for me to finally recognize and understand that.

Like an addict, before I was ready to admit that conflict was negatively impacting my life, I had to hit rock bottom . . . and I hit the bottom, *hard*. I was always a great individual performer, so the problems didn't really start for me until later in my career, when I became responsible for managing others. My approach of "Do what I tell you, when I tell you, how I tell you, or get the fuck out," did not make me popular. Effective maybe, but not popular. People referred to me as "intimidating," which I never understood. Me, intimidating? I thought it was a joke. But in that time in my life, I was like gasoline looking for a match. Often that match was a customer with a problem or concern, or my boss with a critique, question, or suggestion. The old me—defending to the end, and winning at all costs—won most battles, but lost all wars. It started costing me jobs. One job after another, until one day I finally broke down. I had a crisis of confidence. In that moment, I was defeated. With my head in my hands and tears in my eyes, and after spending my entire life in a single profession, I wasn't sure that I could continue to support my family. Making matters worse, in a conversation with my wife, she admitted that she and my son were afraid of me, because I had become so explosive. Think about that for a moment. Who would want that to be true of them? It *was* true of me.

Somehow, what had protected me so well in the past—the fight for survival—had become destructive in my life. It had protected me and others. My colleagues told me all the time, "If the building's on fire, you're in charge." I've always been good in an emergency. It must work like muscle memory or practice, which I had plenty of. I've never been much of a golfer—no one who watched me play would ever call what I do on a golf course golf—but those that do tell me the thing that keeps them coming back is that one good shot. My self-survival response was like that one good shot. The difference for me, though, was that it was my only shot. I applied it in every situation, necessary or not. But boy, did it work well in a crisis. Trouble is, in order for that skill to be valuable, *there had to be a crisis.*

I remember one cold day, when I was around ten years old. My mother and stepfather were working and I was home alone. My dog, Benji, a Miniature Shetland Sheepdog, had gotten loose and fallen through the ice on the pond behind the house. I saw him struggling to climb out of the water, and the ice just kept breaking around him. I initially took a couple of steps out on the ice. But as I got closer to Benji, the ice under me started to crack. I was able to make it back to the shore safely, but Benji was still in danger. I recalled that our neighbor's ten-foot Jon Boat was chained to our deck, and the oars were in the shed. I found the key to the lock, dragged the boat to the edge of the water, used the oars to break the ice, while simultaneously rowing closer to Benji. I was able to reach him and pull him into the boat before something unthinkable happened. In hindsight, I realize I could have easily fallen through the ice and maybe even drowned that day. But thankfully, my self-survival instincts kept me, and Benji, safe.

Much later in life, those survival skills were tested again. This time it was my son in danger. He was in his early teens at the time. One late Saturday afternoon, I was winding down from a long week. It was about 4:30 in the afternoon, just prior to dusk. There was a blizzard warning in effect, and we were expecting one to two feet of snow. My son had gone outside to get some fresh air. We live in a rural area on a few acres with a land preserve of several hundred acres behind us. It had been about forty-five minutes since he went outside, so I searched the yard for him through the windows. I couldn't find him, so I asked my wife if she knew where he was. She said she didn't. I immediately felt like something was wrong. My wife took our St. Bernard out to help locate our son. She walked the perimeter of the property, but speculated that our son had walked down to the pond a few streets away. She put the dog back in the house and got the car out of the garage to drive the neighborhood to find him.

For some reason, it didn't make sense to me that our son had walked to the water. My instincts told me he was lost in the woods. The snow was coming down pretty hard by this point and it was getting dark. The woods were thick and scattered with sinkholes full of water. My fear was that he might have gotten lost, injured, or could potentially freeze to death. Frostbite was another danger. My son had no survival training. Having spent three years in the United States Army Infantry, I had experience living off the land and surviving the elements. My training immediately kicked in. I always travel with cold weather gear, just in case I break down in a remote area. I grabbed the gear out of the car; suited up; and grabbed a flashlight, a compass, my phone, and a SwissTool Victorinox multi-tool. Time was the enemy, so I didn't take the time to charge my Icom two-way radio or search for a first-aid kit.

As soon as I got beyond the edge of the property, I could see tracks entering the woods. I knew then he was in the woods, lost. I called my wife to let her know I found the tracks, and that I would stay with them until I found him. As I followed the tracks, they led through sinkholes full of water, and then I knew he was wet and cold. At some points, the tracks doubled back and went in circles, telling me he was disoriented. I tried to trace the tracks at a full run, while restraining myself from flying into a panic. Every fourth or fifth step, I called out his name. As I was tracking him, I hadn't noticed, but I had lost cell coverage, so I couldn't keep my wife updated. She had called the police and they dispatched a search and rescue team. His tracks were still fresh and visible, but he had traveled through areas that were not yet snow covered. At some points, the tracks faded in and out. When I'd lose them, I'd stop, close my eyes, and take a breath, telling myself that they were there, and I would find him.

My heart was pounding and my mind was racing. What would I find? Each time, I re-acquired the tracks and continued to track him. Suddenly, in the distance, a fence came into view. His tracks led toward the backyard of a house. The tracks went around front and up to the front door. I was relieved that he had found shelter. When I rang the bell, I learned that he wasn't there. He had asked the owner for the address, but not assistance. He used the address to orient himself back to our house. When I made it back to our house, the police were there, and he was already inside covered with blankets. I'm not sure he understood how dangerous that situation was for him. Ultimately, I didn't need to rescue him, he figured it out for himself. But I wasn't far behind and I wouldn't have stopped until I found him.

There's a saying that goes: "What makes someone good, also makes them bad." The idea is that a strength too strong can become a weakness, or highlight imbalance. The proverb, "If all you have is a hammer, everything looks like a nail," is an apt characterization of one's tendency to deploy proven skills when faced with adversity. Inexplicably, I had crossed some invisible threshold that turned my proven skill—self-survival—into self-destruction. And while valuable for others at least twice in my life, most often, during the course of the everyday, being hyper-vigilant is a detriment. Not only for me, but everyone around me. I had to do an honest assessment of how conflict was negatively impacting my life—see Appendix.

—How Conflict is Negatively Impacting My Life—

- *Feel like I'm in one endless argument*
- *Thankless job*
- *Thankless life*
- *Broken relationships*
- *Success at the expense of others*
- *Loss of job, income*
- *Loss of professional confidence*
- *Doubt my ability to continuously provide for my family*
- *Wife and Son afraid of me*

Writing *Wife and Son afraid of me* and seeing it on paper, admitting that it was real and destructive, that's the moment that I knew something had to change. But I had no idea how to change it. Then I received an email from an old colleague, inviting me to dinner. Over dinner he talked about a project he was working on, explaining it was ramping up fast, and that they would need more people. He said it was unlike any other project he'd worked on in the past. It wasn't consulting, it wasn't process improvement, it was coaching.

As part of the work necessary to become a certified professional coach (CPC) with the Institute of Professional Excellence in Coaching (iPEC), students are assigned peers to coach, and are coached by peers as well. My Peer Coach had a particular fluency in working through emotional and intuitive blocks. These blocks are things we feel are limiting us in life. During one conversation, while we were discussing my block (*I'm Not Good Enough*) and I was trying to reconnect with the buried emotions of my abandonment, a picture of a little boy—arms out-stretched, crying and alone—popped into my head. At that regressed moment, I saw myself vulnerable and afraid. I remember explaining to my Peer Coach that after crying, I got angry and decided there and then, that no one would ever put me in that situation again. I armed myself against others as a child in an effort to survive, and in that very instant, ensured I'd experience perpetual conflict.

Recently, I've had the opportunity to start over. Not in the religious sense, but in the do-over, mulligan, fresh start kind of sense. I'm learning how to begin anew, unburdened by the baggage I carried throughout a lifetime. Freed of blaming myself for being abandoned, and unbound from the rage that resulted. A real chance of becoming a whole person, finally feeling like *I'm good enough*.

I've learned that every interaction with another human being is an opportunity to build them up or tear them down. I'm sorry to say, for most of my life, I tore people down. When they put me in the ground—I'm getting to the age that that could be any time—I don't want to be remembered for succeeding at the expense of others. The most encouraging thing about managing conflict is that it is a learnable skill. It's simply a matter of connecting some dots. The remainder of this book will focus on connecting those dots. And when those dots connect, you'll be left with a choice. Now that I know how to change, do I *want* to?

REALITY: BROKEN RULES, BROKEN LIFE

"We don't see things as they are, we see things the way we are."
—Anais Nin

We each have an operational philosophy: our mission orientation, our approach to life, our modus operandi. As such, we all seek out circumstances that reinforce those beliefs, and ignore those that don't. Much has been written about this tendency, and it is referred to as *confirmation bias*. In *What is Art*, Leo Tolstoy wrote: "I know that most men—not only those considered clever, but even those who are very clever, and capable of understanding most difficult scientific, mathematical, or philosophic problems—can very seldom discern even the simplest and most obvious truth if it be such as to oblige them to admit the falsity of conclusions they have formed, perhaps with much difficulty—conclusions of which they are proud, which they have taught to others, and on which they have built their lives."

For most of my life, I followed this operational philosophy:

- *Life is hard;*
- *People suck;*
- *There isn't enough;*
- *Things can't change;*
- *I can't break through;*
- *I'm not good enough.*

Just as Tolstoy suggested, I was blind to the fact that it could be any different. I remember, during iPEC's Life and Leadership Potentials Training, being asked by one of the Instructor Coaches after sharing one of my operational imperatives (Life is hard), "What if it wasn't?" I think I responded with something like: "Yea well, that would be great if it wasn't. But it is, so it doesn't matter." Now, as I'm writing this, I'm sure I can guess what was in her head when she heard my response. It's probably the same thing that's in mine when I hear similar responses from the people I work with.

The thing I'm most grateful to iPEC for is opening my eyes to the fact that I was the source of the conflict in my life. By the end of that initial three-day weekend, a new hope grew within me. I slowly began to flush the old rules that were limiting me, and welcomed new ones: I'm learning about myself; I'm learning about others; I'm growing as a result. And that's when things started to change for me. I stopped getting in my own way, I stopped being the source of my own conflict, my work became more rewarding and fulfilling, my working relationships improved, my performance skyrocketed, and I'd never been more effective.

But first, I had to shine a light on how my Life's Rules weren't serving me. I was serving them, for a life term! In order to manage them, disable them, and eliminate the control they had over me, I had to identify them, along with the behavior that resulted.

One of my rules was: People Suck. If explaining in behavioral terms how I behaved in keeping with that belief, it might sound like: I naturally expect the worst in people. Therefore, I am slow to trust; I prefer to compete rather than cooperate; I expect people to try to take anything from me that I'll allow them to, so I'm eternally on guard. If they are kind to me, they must want something or have some hidden agenda. Nobody does what's best for others, they do what's best for themselves—see Appendix.

The point of going through the exercise was to identify the boundaries we all put ourselves in. In *The Anatomy of Peace* by The Arbinger Institute, they talk about the boxes we build for ourselves this way: "I can put all the effort I want into trying to build my relationships, but if I'm in the box while I'm doing it, it won't help much. If I'm in the box while I'm trying to learn, I'll only end up hearing what I want to hear. And if I'm in the box while I'm trying to teach, I'll invite resistance in all who listen."

Ultimately, we must each decide if our Life's Rules serve us. By serving us I mean, are they healthy and positive, and are they as we would want them to be? If our rules no longer have a place in our lives because they are limiting or negative, then we must make a conscious choice to change them. Otherwise, we risk *serving them* in a quasi-life-sentence kind of way. Much like managing conflict itself, managing our Life's Rules begins by first identifying them.

REASON: HISTORY, INFLUENCING THE PRESENT

"Knowing yourself is the beginning of all wisdom."
—Aristotle

When I began this book, I began by writing that there was a time in my life that I felt like I was in one endless argument. I felt that way because I didn't seem to possess the fundamental ability to get along with others. That inability left me feeling alone, confused, and defective. It didn't make sense to me that others were able to peacefully coexist, but I couldn't. What was wrong with me? Why were others able to navigate similar challenging interpersonal situations without the widespread destruction, and I wasn't able to? It seemed like I had some deeper, more intense connection to the stimulus, a hypersensitivity, that led to a more extreme reaction. So, in addition to learning to manage the conflict itself—by discovering when one's values are offended—I needed to understand why my reactions were so over-the-top, batshit crazy. I needed to know why I seemingly didn't have the internal wiring to control them. A little like my mild dyslexia, which often led to me remembering things, such as phone numbers, backwards.

One day, I was recounting my struggles with conflict to one of the Coachee's I was working with. They were having similar struggles and were interested in how I was able to work through it. Before getting to work through it though, they had to know that conflict negatively impacted my life, providing me the impetus to seek a resolution. After the session had ended, I was thinking about my description: that the abandonment I had experienced as a child wounded me, and resulted in me arming myself against the world. Since that experience, until I ultimately worked through it almost a half-century later, I had been operating in a kind of perpetual self-survival mode, perceiving threats at every turn, regardless of whether they were truly threatening. The self-survival approach, while valuable when it really equaled keeping me safe, had outlived its usefulness. Problem was, though, I was stuck that way. I didn't know any other way of operating. Like any other strength allowed to become too strong, what was once advantageous, fast became an obvious weakness and a liability.

In an effort to better understand the dynamics at play, I began doing research. I happened along an article written by Susan Anderson, the author of *The Journey from Abandonment to Healing: Surviving through and recovering from the five stages that accompany the loss of love.* In Susan's article from 2013, titled "Post Traumatic Stress Disorder of Abandonment, Part 1: An Overview and List of 30 Characteristics," she talks about the idea of post traumatic stress disorder *induced* by abandonment.

In the beginning of the article, Susan writes:

"Following an abandonment experience in childhood or adulthood, some people develop a sequela of post traumatic symptoms which share sufficient features with post traumatic stress disorder to be considered a subtype of this diagnostic category." She continues with an explanation of the condition: "Post Traumatic Stress Disorder (PTSD) is a disease of the amygdala—the emotional center of the brain responsible for initiating the Fight Flee Freeze response. In PTSD, the amygdala is set on overdrive to keep us in a perpetual state of hyper-vigilance, action-ready to declare a state of emergency should it perceive any threat even vaguely reminiscent of the original trauma. The amygdala, acting as the brain's warning system, is constantly working to protect (overprotect) us from any possibility of further injury. In the post trauma related specifically to abandonment, the amygdala scans the environment for potential threats to our attachments to our sense of self." She continues by describing how PTSD of abandonment manifests itself in the lives of the people suffering from it: "People with PTSD of abandonment can have heightened emotional responses to abandonment triggers that are often considered insignificant by others. For instance, depending on circumstances, when we feel slighted, criticized, or excluded, it can instigate an emotional hijacking and jeopardize our personal and professional life."

When I first read those words, I thought she could be writing about me. I fully understood then how, when working with some of my Coachees, they'd tell me: "You just described my life." She was describing in vivid detail the everyday struggles I'd experienced with conflict. I *was* subject to emotional hijackings, many times, daily. It *did* jeopardize my personal and professional life, as well as those around me.

In her article, Susan refers to Daniel Goleman (best known as the author of *Emotional Intelligence: Why It Can Matter More Than*

IQ) and his work around his idea of emotional hijacking. As Susan describes:

> "Once our abandonment fear is triggered, it can lead to what Daniel Goleman calls emotional hijacking. During an emotional hijacking, the emotional brain has taken over, leaving its victims feeling a complete loss of control over their own lives, at least momentarily. If emotional hijacking occurs frequently enough, its chronic emotional excesses can lead to self-depreciation and isolation and give rise to secondary conditions such as chronic depression, anxiety, obsessive thinking, negative narcissism, and addiction."

Susan identifies the more destructive symptoms of the disorder this way:

> "PTSD of abandonment is a psychobiological condition in which earlier separation traumas interfere with current life. An earmark of this interference is intrusive anxiety which often manifests as a pervasive feeling of insecurity—a primary source of self sabotage in our primary relationships and in achieving long range goals. Another earmark is a tendency to compulsively reenact our abandonment scenarios through repetitive patterns, i.e., adandoholism—being attracted to the unavailable.
>
> Another factor of abandonment post trauma is for victims to be plagued with diminished self esteem and heightened vulnerability within social contexts (including the workplace) which intensifies their need to buttress their flagging ego strength with defense mechanisms which can be automatically discharged and whose intention is to protect the narcissistically injured self from further rejection, criti-

cism, or abandonment. These habituated defenses are often maladaptive to their purpose in that they can create emotional tension and jeopardize our emotional connections."

Following her analysis, Susan lists thirty characteristics of post traumatic stress disorder of abandonment, six of which I believed I routinely experienced:

- Difficulty working through the ordinary levels of conflict and disappointment within adult relationships.
- Extreme sensitivity to perceived rejections, exclusions, or criticisms.
- An excessive need for control, whether it's about the need to control others' behavior and thoughts, or about being excessively self-controlled; a need to have everything perfect and done your way.
- Tendency to have unrealistic expectations and heightened reactivity toward others such that it creates conflict and burns bridges to your social connections.
- Co-dependency issues in which you give too much of yourself to others and feel you don't get enough back.
- Tendency toward unpredictable outbursts of anger.

Learning that my defect had a name, a source, characteristics, and symptoms that I could relate to was unbelievably cathartic and empowering. While it might sound fastidious, for me the difference between the idea of being systemically broken and being overreactive due to prior circumstances was a meaningful distinction.

Discovering Anderson's concept of post traumatic stress disorder of abandonment provided me with renewed vigor and hope. As profoundly uplifting as I found that to be, I felt if I continued to educate myself, I might be able to materially impact my ability to get along with others. I was convinced I could learn my way out. People limit themselves in life, personally and professionally, based on their inability to interact with others. It was clear that that was true for me, but as we say in coaching: "It may be normal and natural, but it's not necessary." Now I was convinced that with enough time and effort, I could change that fact, about myself.

Fortunately, during all this, I had been blessed to be making a living as a Coach, working with twenty-two companies and their two thousand five hundred employees in seven states. The work provided me with a steady stream of challenges, none more so than working with people within those companies struggling with organizational change. Those collective experiences led me to my next discovery, a concept called a Super Wicked Problem. Much like learning about PTSD of abandonment, learning about a Super Wicked Problem was the next big step forward.

RESPONSIBILITY:
THE SUPER WICKED PROBLEM

"If not us, who? If not now, when?"
—John F. Kennedy

People ask me all the time, usually in a whisper: "How do things really change?" Generally, I let the question hang a moment, to see if the questioner goes on to offer an answer. Then, breaking the silence and trying to offer the words as though they were a soothing ointment to a fresh burn, I say: "You change them." Their reaction is always the same . . . first, the face contorts by virtue of surprise hijacking their expression; next, the derisive sneer, followed by the look that all but says: "No, you must not have understood the question." Disgust then follows, evidencing the distasteful thoughts stifling the very actions necessary to change things, leading to the dilemma. In this case, it's a personal or professional dilemma; borne out of conflict. That is, they aren't at peace personally or professionally. The individuals seeking change feel disempowered or fearful with respect to their individual ability to positively impact the situation. So they do nothing, allowing dysfunction, negativity, and fear to prevail; perpetuating their own stagnation and, in a way, contributing to it. Edmund Burke, the Irish statesman, once said: "Nobody made a greater mistake than he who did nothing because he could do only a little."

I thought a long while about how to characterize and express this idea of feeling personally or professionally trapped—being victimized by virtue of belonging. Then I remembered a conversation I had with a fellow Coach who was talking about the challenges she faced, with respect to change in her own organization. In doing so, she shared a few examples, and then asked me if I was familiar with the term *wicked problem*. As I was not, she went on to explain: "Problems can be classified as difficult, complicated, complex, and wicked. Difficult problems," she continued, "are those where a clear understanding of the problem exists, and there is consensus about the solution. The only thing missing is action. Complicated problems are those requiring social agreement and technical expertise, like sending a man to the moon," she said. "Complex problems are a little trickier," she continued, "because there is really no one 'right' answer. Raising a child, for instance," she clarified. "But wicked problems," she explained, in a manner that indicated that the mere thought of them exhausted her, "are those problems that defy definition."

I decided to do a little research about wicked problems and learned that C. West Churchman, an American philosopher, systems scientist, professor of business administration, and professor of peace and conflict studies at University of California, Berkeley, first used the term referring to a seminar presented by Professor Horst Rittel. Rittel later teamed with UC Berkeley fellow professor Melvin M. Webber to jointly author *Dilemmas in a General Theory of*

Planning, in which ten characteristics were determined to define a wicked problem. Of the ten, characteristic number eight was particularly instructive for me, with respect to contemplating cultural change. "Every wicked problem can be considered to be a symptom of another problem." Often, a company's culture is a by-product of, and impacted by, other attitudes, behaviors, and policies set forth by leadership, making the cultural manifestation the symptom but not the root cause. Following the work of Rittel and Webber, Russell L. Ackoff, Anheuser-Busch professor emeritus of management science at the Wharton School, University of Pennsylvania, offered his own classification of problems as "messes" in *Systems, Messes, and Interactive Planning*. Later in, *New Tools for Resolving Wicked Problems: Mess Mapping and Resolution Mapping Processes*, Robert Horn, building on Ackoff's work, expanded on the idea of messes and conceived of "social messes." Social messes have fourteen of their own defining characteristics and might be thought of as combinations of problems and messes, or "compound messes." I found the following four characteristics of social messes to be most relevant in the context of cultural change, by virtue of their nature to complicate and stratify cultural dynamics:

- *Most problems are connected to other problems;*
- *Multiple value conflicts;*
- *Great resistance to change;*
- *Problem solver(s) out of contact with the problems and potential solutions.*

Most recently, K. Levin, B. Cashore, Steven Bernstein, and G. Auld of the World Resources Institute paid homage to Rittel and Webber in *Playing it Forward: Path Dependency, Progressive Incrementalism, and the 'Super Wicked' Problem of Global Climate Change* by expanding their work, adding four more characteristics to the original ten. One of the most vexing characteristics of a super wicked problem is number three: "those seeking to solve the problem are also causing it."

We've all heard the old adage: "You're either part of the problem or part of the solution." That adage, while apt, is at the same time somewhat naïve and lacking. It fails to imagine that one could be both part of the problem *and* the solution, each requiring membership. That simultaneous membership is what makes the problem/solution issue so intractable. Divesting the problem or the solution, requires a sacrifice of sorts, a cost. Often, in the case of culture, that cost is too great for a single individual. Hence, a stalemate occurs.

To illustrate, take the consumer adoption curve. When a product or service is first released, the first group of purchasers, Innovators, share a high risk tolerance and are willing to pay a premium for a good or service, but often suffer inconsistent service or goods of unproven quality. The next group, Early Adopters, are slightly more risk averse, demand a little more value, and have higher expectations of service and quality. On a relative basis, Early Adopters tend to get more for their money than the Innovators. Fast forward to the end. The last group, Laggards, enjoy the highest quality product or service, experience the least risk, and derive the most value for money. The lesson here is that delaying action pays the most dividends and becomes its own kind of incentive. Culturally, it works similarly, as the cost is front-loaded. The first to act pays the most. Hence, there is an incentive to wait. The waiting perpetuates the condition, and in that sense, the person waiting to act is contributing to the problem.

No wonder the attempt to change a culture within a company is often viewed as a suicide mission. We've determined that, by characteristics alone, cultural change could be defined as a "super wicked, socially messy problem," hazardous for anyone attempting to intervene and rewarding for those who don't try. This brings to mind the work done by Martin Seligman and his dogs, leading to his theory of learned helplessness. That is, "a perceived absence of control over the outcome of a situation," precluding action of any kind on one's behalf. If that notion is not disempowering enough, through vicarious learning or modeling, it has been found that one person can learn helplessness from another, simply by observing them encountering uncontrollable events. In that sense, helplessness is contagious; it reinforces inaction, and it promotes being stuck.

Will Rogers famously said: "When you find yourself in a hole, the first thing to do is stop digging." That's sage advice, particularly with respect to contributing to a problem. Step One: Recognize you are contributing to a problem. Step Two: Stop contributing. That approach is simply controlling the controllable.

Whether changing an organization or changing yourself, it begins with controlling the controllable. That's you and your own behavior. As you learn more about yourself and your own situation, what's controllable expands. Following that expansion, you will engage each and every encounter on your own terms. That is, coming to view every experience as an opportunity to stretch yourself beyond your comfort zone, knowing each interaction is a gift and a chance to learn and grow.

REALIZE: PEOPLE AND
PERSONAL VALUES

"Values are like fingerprints. Nobody's are the same,
but you leave 'em all over everything you do"
—Elvis Presley

When people ask me what I do, I answer that I work as a
Coach. Inevitably, I get questions like: "Really? What
sport?" I reply: "No, not that kind of Coach. A certified professional coach."

"Oh," they say. "A life coach." The way they say life coach,
though, is revealing. They stretch out the word *life*. It's also usually accompanied by eye rolling, shifting body language, and
quick glances around the room for someone else that might offer a
conversation that requires less work. In truth, I'm not really a life
coach; that designation is a little too broad. I specialize in individual and group conflict. The fact that I lived full-scale conflict
every day for most of my life has made me an expert working with
it, and now it's true that I'm at my absolute best with people who
are at their absolute worst.

Individually, conflict impacts one's personal interactions, professional interactions, and performance. In a group context, conflict impacts relationships; stifling communication, destroying teamwork, and promoting the creation and perpetuation of dysfunctional and destructive cultures. I usually leave out that part, though. It precludes the blank stares, the uncomfortable silence, and the search for an inevitably awkward response. It reminds me of the reaction I used to get when I worked as a facilitator. Most often, that was interpreted as a veiled term to mean "unemployed." While Coach is not quite as abstruse as Facilitator, it's still not quite conversationally friendly. Based on those types of responses, I've since tweaked my reply. Now when asked what I do, I simply reply, "I work with conflict."

Helping people manage conflict out of their lives starts with them learning about their own personal values. Learning that:

- All human behavior is a function of personal values.
- If you don't understand someone else's behavior, you don't understand their personal values.

People have a hard time wrapping their heads around the idea of personal values. Values are simply what's important or meaningful to us, at the deepest level. It's our BIOS, or basic input/output system. Our individual programming necessarily informs our behavior. It colors our world and becomes the filter through which we see life. Our values manifest themselves in our everyday life and overall existence. They appear in what we drive, where we live and work, who we live and work with, what we wear, where we shop, and which groups we belong to. Collectively, our values become our own internal algorithm, a formulaic composite of our "go to market (life) strategy." They operate as our rudder, and they keep us on course in challenging times. The fact is, if I had enough time to follow people around and watch their behavior from a distance, I wouldn't have to ask them their values . . . I could tell them.

- Our personal values become the method by which we measure ourselves and others.
- Our personal values serve as our ideals, and also our judgments.

During iPEC's certified professional coach training, I remember having to declare my personal values. I remember being almost paralyzed by the question. My nature is to be deliberative, so when faced with BIG questions, I tend to respond S-L-O-W-L-Y. Being provided a list to select from helped a lot, and so I chose achievement, autonomy, connecting to others, family, and personal growth. They asked us to call someone close to us and ask them a word that that person would use to describe us. I reached out to my youngest brother-in-law, and he responded with integrity.

In the beginning, I used a list with my Coachees as well, thinking it would make the task a little easier for them. It did. But it also resulted in some people highlighting almost every word offered, because at one time or another in their life, they felt like they exemplified that trait. So now, in an effort to make our time together most valuable and productive, I've learned to approach the conversation in a different way. I begin the conversation by requesting:

- "Pretend you're describing yourself to a stranger, and you'd like that stranger to know everything about you that you'd want them to know, in six, eight, or ten words. What are those words?"—see Appendix.

They'll usually think about it for a moment, and then start providing me with their words. Occasionally, they'll ask me for a little guidance. When they do, I ask them to think about a brand that they have strong feelings about. For example, Mercedes Benz might translate to prestige and power; BMW might translate to luxury, performance, and status; Audi might translate to precision and refinement, etc. I ask them to tell me the words that that brand means to them. Once they do that, I suggest that that is what they are doing with respect to themselves. "Okay, I understand now," they'll say, and then give me their words.

Recently, I worked with a young man who chose the following words: successful, passionate, trustworthy, hardworking, selfless, competitive, caring, thoughtful, generous, and positive. What he was doing, but didn't realize, was:

- declaring his personal values.

By declaring those values, he was taking the first step towards managing the conflict that was negatively impacting his life.

STEP ONE–DECLARING PERSONAL VALUES

"Knowledge isn't power until it is applied."
—Dale Carnegie

The purpose of this book is to help those who have repeatedly experienced conflict negatively impacting their lives. Such could be evidenced by a string of broken relationships, divorce, job loss, propensity for violent arguments, and outbursts.

My second intention is to help people *impacted* by those struggling with conflict directly—my wife and my son, for example—and help them better understand the underpinnings of the negative behavior. Those impacted most are the closest. They are the first responders and can easily become part of the collateral damage. They may want to assist, but without comprehending the dynamics of what's at play, will be left confused, afraid, overwhelmed, and feeling powerless—or worse, done with trying to help and ready to hit the exit. For the impacted, understanding the nature of conflict is essential. It gives them hope and confidence. Hope that they can do some good, and the confidence to positively impact a situation they would like to be different.

In reading the subsequent exchanges, I'd like you to think about the dialogue from two points of view. First, the Coachee's perspective—the person directly struggling with conflict. Can you relate to what they are saying? Have you felt that way? Have you said those words? Second, the Coach's perspective—the person actively attempting to help the Coachee become self-aware. Try to understand the concepts well enough to be able to deliver them in a way that will make a material difference in the behavior of that other person.

There are hundreds more examples I could provide, but ultimately they are all the same. Behavior follows values. The stories of Marty, David, Melissa, and Stacy help us understand.

Personal Values and Value's Driven Behavior—I

Prior to leaving any client location, the last thing I do is schedule my next visit. The conversation generally turns to one of focus for next time. In this particular case, I was at a car dealership, and the general manager and I were discussing the plan for that next visit. When he asked me in to his office and closed the door behind me, I realized he had something on his mind.

"I'd like you to work with Marty," he said.

"Marty, the Parts Department manager Marty?"

"Yes."

"Okay, sure," I answered. "What's going on with him?"

"He doesn't get along with anyone in the building," he said. "If it doesn't change, I'm going to have to let him go. His behavior is causing too much disharmony and disruption. I've talked to him about it—more than once, actually—but nothing has changed. So, I figured you're the Coach. What's your specialty again?"

"Conflict," I said.

"Exactly," he exclaimed. "Conflict. So, you deal with him." He smiled. "You have the tools, the training, and the experience to get through to this guy. I'm done trying. It's finally gotten to the point that I can't work with him like this anymore. I have to do something about it. I've put up with it all this time, because he's good at his job. But enough is enough, you know. Being good at your job doesn't justify being a complete asshole all the time. I mean, NOBODY in the building wants to deal with him. I've just let it go on for way too long, to the point that it's now too destructive to the rest of the operation. So, I want you to work with him, and see if we can salvage him. If not, he's out. How's that?"

"Of course, I'll give you and Marty, my best," I replied. "I'll see you next month." I then circulated around the building saying my good-byes.

I was glad to have some time to prepare for what I knew could be a difficult conversation with Marty. I wanted to be sure that he didn't feel like he was being personally attacked when we addressed the issues surrounding his relationships with his co-workers. I came up with a game plan, and we met as scheduled.

Each coaching interaction begins with me getting to know the Coachee, and it's not something that can be rushed. There has to be an element of trust between the Coachee and the Coach, without which no progress can be made. Marty and I took the time necessary, and when it felt right, we got to work.

"So, I was pleased when Tom asked me to spend a little time with you today, Marty. I know we haven't done much of that in the past, so, I was glad to be given an opportunity to get to know you a little better. I'm going to begin by asking you a question that you may find a little weird, at first. Please know though, I ask it the way I do on purpose. I've found it's the easiest and most effective way to go about it, without tainting your response. I promise, I'll explain it fully afterwards," I assured. "But, for now, I'm going to ask you to think about it just the way I've asked you to. Are you okay with that?"

"Sure, I can do that," he said.

"Great, thank you," I replied. "Here goes, then. Marty, I'd like you to pretend you were describing yourself to a stranger, and you'd like that stranger to know everything about you that you'd want them to know about you, in six, or eight, or ten words. What are those words?"

"Can you say that again, slower?" he requested.

"Of course," I said, and then repeated the request more slowly.

"Okay, got it that time," he said. "Thank you." Marty took several minutes to jot down a few of his words. When he was finished, I asked him to share his words with me. "I'm always on time," he said. "I'm dependable. If you need me to work, I'm going to work. I'm honest, trustworthy, and good at my job."

"Okay, great, thank you for that," I said. "Marty, in your description of yourself, I heard timeliness/promptness, dependability, work ethic, commitment, honesty, trustworthiness, competence . . . is there anything else you'd like to add?"

"I care about my job," he offered. "I've been here a long time, and it's close to home. I don't want to work anywhere else."

"Well, based on that, Marty, it sounds like you really, truly value your job," I observed.

"I do," he confirmed.

"Marty, would you say that, when you are faced with a given situation, you have to give it serious thought, and think about being honest and trustworthy . . . like it's a carefully considered choice, or by default, in every situation, you are honest and trustworthy?"

Marty laughed. "No, I'm honest and trustworthy pretty much all the time. Even some times I shouldn't be," he joked.

"How about promptness and being dependable?" I primed. "Marty, tell me about a time when you were not prompt and dependable."

I could tell he was a little puzzled. After pausing for a moment,

Marty said, "There's really not a time when I'm not prompt and dependable. I guess it's just the way I'm wired," he confessed.

"So, would you be more likely to say to someone: I behave dependably, or *I am dependable?*"

"I would say: I *am* dependable. Aren't they the same thing, though?"

"Yes and no," I replied. "It has to do with how closely you identify that characteristic of yourself to *who you are,* rather than *what you do.* And it can complicate something, but we'll talk about that in a little bit. That aside though, it sounds like you closely identify with being dependable. Like it's *part of you, part of who you are . . .* part of your personal brand."

"It is part of who I am," he said, affirming.

"I'm glad to hear you say that, Marty. Would you say that at all times, and in all cases, you are those other things that you mentioned as well?"

"Yes, I would say that, also" he acknowledged.

"Okay, great, that's perfect," I acknowledged. "Earlier, I said that I would fully explain the point of the question, so, here's the explanation. When I asked you to describe yourself to a stranger, and you gave me your words, what you were really doing—unknowingly—is declaring your personal values," I shared. "As I mentioned beforehand, I ask about them, and specifically that way, because some people have difficulty talking about them directly. For some people, it can be too big a question, and it becomes difficult for them to answer in a short period of time."

"Makes sense," he said.

"And your values manifest in your behavior," I stated.

"Mana-what?"

"They are present, they are represented in, they are demonstrated by, they are evident, visually," I said. "If I followed you around, Marty, would you say that I would see you being prompt, dependable, trustworthy, honest, committed, hardworking, and caring?"

"Yes."

"Sometimes, most times, or all the time?"

"All the time," he said.

"So can we agree, then, that your behavior is in keeping with your personal values always?"

"Sure," he said. "We can agree on that."

"I'm glad," I began. "Because I truly believe that if I were to follow someone around for any length of time, I would be able tell them their personal values based on their behavior. I wouldn't have to ask them. How about for you, Marty? What about others? Do you believe that other people behave in keeping with their values all the time?"

He hesitated a moment. After some consideration, he answered, "I guess it happens with everyone, the same way as me . . . I just never really thought about it that way before."

"So, does it make sense to you that, if you wanted to understand a little more about your own or someone else's behavior, you might need to better understand their personal values?"

"Yes," he said. "Makes perfect sense to me."

"Okay, I'm pleased that you agree with that," I replied. "So, why do you think that I spend so much time working with people to identify and declare their personal values?"

"Well, we just talked about how it helps people understand their own behavior, right? And those people, understanding other people's behavior too."

"Yes, exactly," I said. "But there's one more big reason," I suggested. "Any guesses?"

"Not a clue."

"Okay, no problem. Before we go forward though, I just want to be sure that I've made my points clearly enough so far." I summed that up for him. "All human behavior is a function of one's personal values. If you don't understand someone else's behavior, you don't understand their personal values and vice-versa."

"Got it," he said, and repeated it back to me.

"Fantastic," I said. "Okay, the other big reason I spend so much time working with people to declare their personal values, is because their personal values *are also their triggers*. Conflict exists when someone feels like one of their personal values has been offended. So any situation that you encounter which challenges one of your personal values—what I refer to as hot situations—will spin you up emotionally. So for you Marty, any situation that you experience that challenges your personal values of timeliness/promptness, dependability, work ethic, commitment, honesty, trustworthiness, competence, or caring will become an emotional event in your life. And that happens when someone challenges you *being* one of those things—like someone saying you're not honest, for example—or when you witness someone else *not being* those things—like someone not being trustworthy, for instance. There will be situations that are prone to offending your personal values. And, in order to manage those hot situations, you must first be able to identify them. Remember earlier, when I asked you about whether you would say you behaved dependably or you were dependable?"

"Yes," he answered.

"And I said it had to do with complicating something," I reiterated.

"Yes," he said again.

"The complication has to do with the emotional intensity of your reaction to an offended personal value," I said. "That's how much emotion exists to fuel that emotional reaction, when one of your personal values is offended. If you believe and feel that that particular personal value is synonymous with who you are, not just behavior you exhibit, then there will be more emotion that exists than there would be otherwise. So, some situations can be hotter than others, due to depth of your association to that particular personal value that's offended. But, any situation where you feel one of your personal values is offended will be a hot one for you. The challenge is to understand when they occur most, so that you can learn to manage around, or eliminate, the reactions that result. I'd like to explore that with you next." I guided.

"Great," he said, clearly a little anxious. "I can't wait."

"I have one last question before we continue though," I said, preparing him. "How peaceful are your days?" I let that question hang a bit. In between me asking and hearing his response, I was speculating about his answer. I was remembering how far from peaceful my days had been in the past.

His reply confirmed my suspicion. "My day?" he asked, like he was surprised I asked. "My days are not peaceful," he said pointedly. "There's no peace in my day."

Now that Marty had completed Step One, Declaring One's Personal Values, he was ready to better understand how those values were being offended, leading to the conflict he was creating and experiencing in his work and in his life. We'll pick back up with Marty in Step Two, Identifying Hot Situations.

Personal Values and Value's Driven Behavior—II

I was meeting with David (director of parts and service) and his fellow managers to discuss the results of a recent employees' survey. One thing was painfully clear to all: David's scores were the lowest of any manager, and his department's scores were the lowest of all departments. During our meeting, David offered justification after justification and became overly defensive of his approach. It was obvious that there was a serious chasm between David and his employees, and based on our meeting, it appeared to extend to the other managers as well. After the meeting, one of the managers pulled me aside. He wanted me to know that he thought David was a good guy. But deep down, and not so much on the surface.

"David just needs to sit behind a desk and crunch numbers," he suggested. "He can't deal with customers or his employees. When he does, it's a nightmare. You should hear him go after people, it's unbelievable." He summed up David's style. "Winning battles and losing wars."

"How is it with the other managers?" I asked.

"Same," he said. "He protects his turf. With David it's always win/lose, and he's not going to lose. Especially if it has anything to do with an expense or something else that he feels negatively impacts him or his department. He just doesn't want to hear it." As he said this, he was pulling out a sheet of paper. "We actually created a list," he said.

"A list," I repeated, a little unsure of what he meant.

"Yes, we have a list . . . a list of people that will no longer do business here, because they won't do business with David. I wish I was kidding." I could tell he meant it. Ultimately though, after everything was said, he chalked it up to David just being David.

One thing I've learned in my day-to-day work: the person referred to with any of the following prefixes is a person mired in conflict:

- "Oh, that's just (insert name here)" or
- "That's just (so-and-so) being (so-and-so)."

Anytime I hear it, I know the deal, because that's how people used to refer to me. It gave me a pass for being an asshole, an animal, a jerk, and a maniac. It condoned my behavior, because I was good at my job. But, my behavior took a toll on everyone around me, and it destroyed the culture.

Healthy cultures are safe environments. People share their opinions without fear of criticism or retribution, they seek and accept responsibility, and they own their own performances, failures and all. Dysfunctional cultures are rife with silence, finger-pointing, and blame; a charged atmosphere, intolerant of mistakes, unyielding in demands, and preoccupied with finding fault. While I was the one responsible for creating that environment around me, I still suffered from its effects. My self-awareness was zero, so I couldn't see how I was contributing to and perpetuating the dysfunction. I just knew I was performing a thankless job and living a thankless life. I felt like I was in one long argument on a daily basis; either with co-workers, other managers, bosses, or customers, and it continued when I got home at night with my wife.

So, now, I'm tuned in to that description of someone. Because I know that's coded language. Code for what I'd now describe as: That's just a person behaving in keeping with their own personal values. Their behavior is manifestly demonstrative of those personal values. They are intolerant of the personal values of others and impose their personal values on everyone around them. They vigorously defend those personal values against any perceived offense. At its absolute simplest though, it describes someone who has come to be known by others as emotionally reactive. And those emotional reactions are driven and perpetuated by a lack of self-awareness and awareness of others.

During the managers' meeting, David talked about how disappointed he was in his people's motivation levels. He just didn't feel like anyone had the drive that he had, and he felt that they were holding him, and his department, back. He spoke several times of trying to *push and push* but getting no additional results. He talked a lot about his frustration in not being able to get his people to perform at a higher level, despite the fact that he continued to push them. He also spoke about his people's lack of respect of time.

How, in his view, minutes become hours, and hours become days, and days become weeks, etc. This culminated in a time-is-money operational philosophy.

After the initial meeting with all of the managers, I usually met with each, one-on-one. I was pleased that David offered to be first. We took a quick break, grabbed a coffee from the catering truck, and reconvened. As this was only my second time at the dealership, and my first time meeting David one-on-one, we opened with the preliminaries. David explained that he had been in his position for about seven years. He felt he had done a good job "by the metrics." He did feel like he'd hit a performance wall and wasn't sure how to break through. He felt that he was at his lowest point and mentioned that, beyond all the business concerns, he had some family issues going on as well.

Unfortunately, David's personal confession didn't surprise me much. In fact, I would have been more surprised if that weren't the case. People living conflict live it twenty-four-seven, at work, at home, on the golf course, coaching Little League, wherever. It manifests itself in everything. Those of us living it, first put it on like a uniform, but it never comes off. In that sense, it's more like a second permanent skin, protecting us, yet isolating and condemning us at the same time.

"David, during the managers' meeting, you spent a lot time describing the current dynamics," I said. "But, I'm more interested in how you would describe yourself. I'm going to ask you a question that may sound a little curious at first, but I ask it the way I do, and specifically the way I do, purposefully. I've found it to be the best way to elicit the most helpful replies from the people that I work with. So, I'm asking for your indulgence here, to please play along."

"Sure," he said, graciously. "I'd be happy to."

"Okay, thank you," I replied. "I really appreciate it. So here it is. I'd like you to pretend you were describing yourself to a stranger, and you'd like that stranger to know everything about you that you'd want them to know about you, in six, or eight, or ten words. What are those words?"

He thought about it, but only for a moment before replying.

"I work, I make money, I provide for my family. It's pretty simple. That's why I can't understand why my people don't want to do the same thing. Work ethic, time, money."

There was a long period of silence.

"Okay," I said, "tell me—"

But then, David let loose. "All my life, I've worked hard. When I was young, it was a paper route. Then as I got older, it was baseball. If I wasn't playing, I was practicing. If I wasn't practicing, I was playing. I knew I had to work hard to keep my scholarship in college. I pushed and pushed as hard as I could. Always. Again, I know I've said this a couple of times, but I just can't understand why my people don't want more for themselves. Why should I want more for them than they want for themselves? It just doesn't make any sense to me."

It was painfully obvious to me that one of the things David was struggling with was this idea of wanting more for his people than they wanted for themselves. This is the hallmark of a great leader, a great manager, and a great Coach. Seeing in them what those people don't see in themselves, seeing what they can become, in a way that they themselves may be blind to. That outside perspective, that encouraging vision for them, necessarily lifts those people up. It creates something aspirational for them, it helps elevate them and their performance beyond what they believe themselves to be capable of. But, in David's case, there was one critical missing component.

David's "wanting" for his people wasn't something that they wanted for themselves. I knew—based on the comments from his employees who had taken the survey—that his people were striving for more work/life balance, not less. So, his wanting longer hours for them, to elevate their income and their performance, wasn't aspirational for them. It was exactly the opposite of that; it was de-motivational. No amount of David's wanting that for them—that which they didn't want for themselves—would change that. In fact, as he was describing, it quickly became counterproductive. In David's case, his struggle primarily had to do with how he was imposing his own personal values on everyone around him unintentionally. That fact was clearly evidenced during my conversation with him, during which he essentially said (without actually saying it this way), *I can't fathom why people don't act more like I do. I don't understand why their behavior doesn't honor my personal values? I can't comprehend why people don't want more of what I want for them?* That lack of understanding was purely driven by David's lack of self-awareness, and his lack of awareness of others. So the task at hand was to try to help him develop awareness of both self and others.

"David, it sounds like you consider yourself to be driven," I observed.

"Absolutely, I'm driven. In everything I do, all the time."

"Are you ever *not* driven?"

"You don't know me that well," he said, chuckling. "I'M ALWAYS DRIVEN," he said, then proudly proceeded to tell me about a time that has since become legend. "One Christmas," he began, "the kids had already opened their presents, and we had already had our Christmas meal, so I went to work. The place was closed, but there was work that I could I do, things that needed to be done. What was I going to do, sit at home and watch basketball?"

The way he added that last sentence helped me understand that, for him, that was the most absurd and ridiculous thing he could imagine. "Wow," I said. "What did the family think of that?"

"They're used to it," he shrugged. "It didn't surprise them."

"David, when I asked you earlier to pretend you were describing yourself to a stranger, you gave me some words. You said you work, you make money, and you provide for your family. I think we can add driven, as well, after hearing that Christmas story. When you gave me your words, what you were actually doing, unbeknownst to you, was declaring your personal values. All human behavior is a function of one's personal values, and it's clear to me, based on your behavior, that you *are* driven."

"In addition to driving one's behavior," I continued, "personal values play a big part in people's interactions with one another. Personal values can also be a source of conflict and judgement. Conflict exists when someone feels like one of their personal values has been offended. Conflict also exists when someone feels like another is imposing their personal values on them. Both situations can result in us creating the behavior in others that we don't want. I'd like to explore that a little more with you, if that would be okay."

"Fine with me," he said. "Fire away."

Now that David had completed the first step of declaring one's personal values, he was ready to better understand how imposing those personal values on others was leading to the conflict he was creating and experiencing in his work and in his life. We'll pick back up with David in Step Two - Identifying Hot Situations.

Personal Values and Values Driven Behavior—III

"I need you to work with the service advisors today," Eric said. "It's like a war zone down there."

"Hot or cold?" I asked.

"What?"

"You said it's like a war zone down there. A hot war or a cold war?"

"What's the difference?"

"In a hot war, the aggression will be overt. You'll have openly aired disagreements—arguments, basically—along with everything else that comes with that, short of physical altercations. In a cold war, it's a more passive style of aggression. On the surface, things will seem fine, but when someone's back is turned, that's when the damage is done."

"Described like that, it's more cold than hot then," he said. "Melissa hung up on a customer the other day. *Hung up on them.* It's gotten so bad down there that we've come to refer to Mondays as: Melissa's Customer Mondays. Mondays have been the worst. Maybe because we're closed Sunday, so we're dealing with carry-overs from Saturday, or maybe we're overbooking Mondays, but Mondays have been a flat-out nightmare. Those two—Stacy and Melissa—never got along great to begin with, but it's reached a whole new level now. And it's starting to negatively impact our customers, which you know, I can't allow. So, I need you to spend some time with both Stacy and Melissa today and see if you can get that figured out. Other than that, they do a good job, you know. I'd like to be able to keep them both."

"Of course," I said. "I'll meet with them and circle back with you later."

"Sounds like a plan," he said as he was leaving. "I'll catch you before the day's out."

Stacy had some time available, so I started with her.

"Hey, Stacy," I said, as she entered the conference room.

"Good morning," she replied.

"Eric asked me to spend some time with you and Melissa today. So thank you for making time for me."

"No problem. Are we in trouble?" she asked, in a wise-guy kind of way.

"What do you mean, are you in trouble?"

"Well, you usually spend all of your time with the people that 'need it,'" she said, creating air quotes with her hands.

"Nobody's in trouble," I said. "Eric said that it's been challenging on the Drive, and he asked me to meet with you both. I'm anxious to hear what's going on. Are you starting to get comfortable with the job?"

"It's been five months now," she said. "I just now finally feel like I've learned the job. Like I know what to do, and can do those things without having to constantly ask for help. That's made things a little better between me and Melissa."

"How so?"

"Melissa was not that cooperative when I asked her for help," she confided. "She would help me, but she would make it extremely painful. It's payback . . . " she said, trailing off.

"What do you mean, payback?" I asked, genuinely puzzled.

"We worked together at our prior jobs," she explained. "We both came from RW&B Healthcare—Red, White & Blue Healthcare," she said. "I was her boss. I had to train *her* when she got assigned to my department. She got here first, though, so here, it's the other way around."

"Do you think you were hard on her at the last job, when you trained her?"

"Oh, God no," she said. "I did everything I could to help her be successful. That's my nature."

"So, why do you imagine it's different here?"

"I think she feels like I have to pay my dues. Melissa got here a year before I did, and she didn't get hired as a service advisor right away because she didn't have any experience. She was initially hired as a service department assistant, and she had to do grunt work for six or eight months before getting promoted. I think she resents the fact that I got hired in as a service advisor from the beginning. So, I'm sure she feels like I skipped a step. That's why she makes it so painful for me, because in the beginning it was painful for her. So, we don't really get along as well as I'd like."

"And how would you like it to be different?"

"I'd like us to be a team, you know. We're the only women on the Service Drive and we need to stick together more. Watch out for each other."

"Stacy, my specialty is working with conflict between people," I said. "Would it be okay if I shared something with you, that I think might help improve things between you two?"

"Sure," she said. "I would really appreciate that."

"Okay then," I started. "That begins by me asking you a question that some find to be a bit puzzling at first, but I ask it the way I do on purpose. I promise I'll fill in the blanks later. I'd like you to pretend you're describing yourself to a stranger, and you'd like that stranger to know everything you'd want them to know about you, in six, or eight, or ten words. What are those words?"

She was quiet at first. I could tell she was giving it serious thought. "Okay," she said. "I'm ready."

"Okay, shoot," I said, prepared.

"Loving, caring, smart, compassionate, determined, fun, energetic . . . how many is that?"

"Seven," I answered.

"Is that enough?"

"That's perfect," I said. "Exactly what I was looking for. When I asked you to describe yourself to a stranger, Stacy, you gave me your words. Those words are your personal values. So when you answered, you were actually declaring those personal values, without knowing it. The reason it's important to understand one's personal values, is because personal values drive people's behavior. All human behavior is a function of personal values. So if you don't understand someone else's behavior, it means you don't understand their personal values, and vice-versa. Conflict exists, when someone feels like one of their personal values has been offended. Or, if someone feels like another is imposing their personal values on them.

So, any situation you face that challenges the idea of you being loving, caring, smart, compassionate, determined, fun, energetic, or if you witness someone not being those things, that will be a hot situation for you. That is, you will become emotionally charged as a result. That emotional charging will lead to you either suppressing it—you'll withdraw, stop communicating, feeling helpless and powerless—or lash out, becoming angry and aggressive, argumentative and combative. Are you able to relate to that given your situation with Melissa?"

"Yes, absolutely," she said. "Melissa's probably more like the second one you said—lashing out—and I'm probably more like the first one, withdrawing."

"And which personal values come into play for you, Stacy?"

"Well, definitely the loving, caring, and compassion ones anyway," she answered. "Honestly, I do think that Melissa should be more compassionate."

"It would be perfectly natural for you to judge Melissa based on her honoring your personal value of compassion. Personal values influence how we see the world and everything in it. When you say, 'Melissa should be more compassionate,' that's exactly what you are doing. You're judging her based on how compassionate you think she is. Keep in mind though, Stacy, Melissa will only behave compassionately if compassion exists in her personal value structure. If it isn't present, then it won't manifest in her behavior. When she isn't compassionate enough, or she doesn't act compassionately enough, that will offend your personal value of compassion. Because in your world, all people are compassionate, all the time. So, any experience that is counter to that will be a hot situation for you. You'll spin up emotionally, and based on your own identification, you'll react as a Victim. Meaning you'll withdraw, stop communicating, and feel helpless and powerless."

"But at the same time, whatever situation you're experiencing with Melissa—the one leaving you feeling like she *should be more compassionate*—that very situation could have Melissa, who's simply acting on behalf of her own personal values, thinking *you are too compassionate*. Meaning, from her point of view, *you're not whatever*—fill-in-the-blank—*enough,* with respect to her personal values. So, at the very same time you're thinking she's not compassionate enough, she's thinking you're too compassionate. And you both become emotionally reactive based on what you believe the other is either *too much* or *not enough* of. That's what makes this interpersonal stuff so crazy. You're each measuring each other based on your own set of personal values. Both fully expecting the other to honor their respective personal values. And when that doesn't happen, you both spin up emotionally; she lashes out, and you withdraw. But you're doing it to each other. That's the insanity of it. You are each creating the behavior in the other, that neither of you wants."

"Try to think about it this way. Let's say there are a bunch of balloons down there," I said, referencing the Service Drive. "And let's also say her favorite color is red, and yours is blue. And you each choose a balloon. When she chooses her balloon, she chooses a red one, and when you choose yours, you choose blue. Then she's upset with you for choosing the blue one, because she believes red is better than blue, and in turn, you're upset with her, because she chose the red one. In your world blue is better than red. So her balloon isn't blue enough from your perspective, and for her, yours isn't red enough. But the reality is, neither is better. Blue isn't better or worse that red or vice-versa. They each represent the same 'goodness,' but they *are* different. I can't know for sure what's going on for her without talking with her about it, but this happens frequently, especially when people have diametrically opposed personal values, like a clock for example. If your personal values are at twelve o'clock and hers are at six o'clock, then they will be directly opposed. When that's true, the other's behavior will demonstrate the exact opposite of your behavior. For example, one of your stated values was fun, right?"

"Yes," she confirmed.

"Let's say one of Melissa's is dedication then. As such, she might interpret your carefree, enjoy-life, have-fun attitude at work as a lack of dedication. For her, she might feel like you're not taking your job seriously enough. You, on the other hand, might see her as too driven, too rigid, too task oriented . . . too serious. Now, let's say the personal value of another of your co-workers is balance. And let's say balance exists at nine o'clock or three o'clock—again using the clock example—halfway between the two positions of twelve o'clock and six o'clock. That person might value being dedicated and having fun, as one balancing the other. So that person will be less offended, and less emotionally reactive, when faced with situations involving the perceived dichotomy of fun and dedication. And from a balloon perspective, that person would probably have chosen a purple one, if available . . . a blend of red and blue."

"That's probably enough for today, Stacy. I'm going to meet with Melissa next. Once I've had a chance to speak with her, I'd like to meet with you both again, together. We'll do that next time. Between now and then though, I'd like you think about what we covered today. The better able you are to understand your own behavior, and how that behavior is a direct result of your personal values, the better able you will be to recognize that other people's behavior is simply them honoring their personal values. And while you may not share the same personal values with them, none of theirs, or yours, are right or wrong, good or bad; they are just different from each other. So, acknowledging that inherent goodness and difference doesn't mean agreeing with, condoning, adopting, or accepting their values or behavior as your own. It simply means recognizing it for what it is; their personal values drive their behavior. And if we can come to respect each other for our differences, that's a step closer to eliminating the conflict."

And so I met with Melissa. Her initial words were tough, process driven, and personal responsibility; these served to bolster my previous conclusion of the dynamics that were complicating the relationship between her and Stacy. In our conversation, Melissa shared that she felt Stacy wasn't *tough enough* in many situations. In those same situations, Stacy felt Melissa wasn't *compassionate enough*, or was being *too tough*. Each assessed the worth of their own particular personal value more. Neither realized that toughness and compassion are equally valuable, only different. The conversation continued, and I aimed to help Melissa gain a modicum of self-awareness, along with guiding her to achieve some insight with respect to Stacy's behavior. I hoped that added understanding would reduce the perceived offensiveness of the behavior she was witnessing, so that a truce could be called to what had become a close-quarters battle of personal values.

RECURRENCE: PERSONAL VALUES AS TRIGGERS

"When we are no longer able to change a situation—
we are challenged to change ourselves"
—Viktor E. Frankl

Marshall Goldsmith, along with Mark Reiter, recently released a book entitled *Triggers: Creating Behavior That Lasts—Becoming The Person You Want To Be.* Goldsmith is a best-selling author, and best known for *What Got You Here Won't Get You There.* He was also personal coach to Alan Mulally (Ford Motor Company CEO, 2006-2014). In his introduction, Goldsmith calls a trigger "any stimulus that reshapes our thoughts and actions."

"In every waking hour," he writes, "we are being triggered by people, events, and circumstances that have the potential to change us. Our environment is the most potent triggering mechanism in our lives. A trigger can be internal or external. External triggers come from the environment, bombarding our five senses as well as our minds. Internal triggers come from thoughts or feelings that are not connected with any outside stimulus."

Part of my focus is on triggers as well. For me though, with respect to conflict, *triggering happens in a particular way.* In the two prior chapters, we invested the time to learn about the importance of one's personal values and how, relative to them, one's behavior results. It's absolutely essential to identify your personal values, because when declaring your personal values, you are also *identifying your triggers.*

- Conflict exists when someone feels like one of their personal values has been offended.

For example, if one of your personal values is thoughtfulness, then any situation that you encounter that challenges you being thoughtful, or when witnessing another behaving in opposition of that value, you will "spin up" emotionally. Why? Because, in your world, all people are thoughtful, all the time! How dare someone challenge your thoughtful nature! If someone else can't be thoughtful, you want them out of your world. The emotion exists to provide the energy to *act.* In the particular case of conflict, the emotion exists to provide the energy to *react.* The reaction aims to change the situation from what it *is,* to what we want it *to be.* If another is not being thoughtful, it is the energy to confront that situation. If it is a challenge to our own thoughtful nature, the energy will arm the defense. It is the same with any other personal value, and any situation that challenges that personal value; or when we witness another behaving contrary to that personal value, emotional ignition will result.

Based on one's personal values structure, certain situations will be *hot situations.* That is, there will be certain situations that are prone to offending one's personal values. For example, one of my persistent challenges is dealing with someone's behavior that I *interpret* to be inconsiderate. Any situation that I face where I *believe* another is being inconsiderate is a hot situation for me. It can be as little as someone not using a turn signal or not stopping at a stop sign. If I were more rules-based, someone not using their turn signal might offend me in a different way. I might feel like they were flouting the law and being intentionally defiant. But the offense for me is that someone not using a turn signal requires that *I wait for them* to take whatever action it is they are taking, spending precious time that I wouldn't have to if I knew their intentions in advance—I could proceed accordingly. My perception is that their behavior makes me subservient to them, and I am not worthy of their consideration.

Likewise, when someone rolls through a stop sign, they often preclude the advancement of someone else who has been patiently waiting. It sends the message that that other patient party doesn't matter. It invites unhealthy competition.

When someone's invited to compete in that way—the way one behaves when shopping for the last, hard-to-find gift for a child, when the line to checkout is out the door, when the traffic is bumper to bumper during a commute, when there *isn't enough something for too many of us*—one usually does compete, and it often brings out our worst. If we play too hard to win, it results in an unhealthy competition that divides people. Conflict is about interactions that produce winners and losers. It's about succeeding directly at the expense of others. Conflict is about reaction's brought on by emotions. When someone is reactive, they are not their best self, nor do they produce the best outcome, and never the smartest one. So, to summarize:

- By declaring one's personal values, one also identifies their triggers.
- Conflict exists when one feels like one of their personal values has been offended, or when one feels like another is imposing their personal values on them.

- Certain situations are prone to offending one's personal values. One must first identify those hot situations, in order to manage them.

Once more, hot situations are a function of one's values structure. In order to manage those situations, one must first be able to identify them. Much like my work with personal values, I've learned to ask about hot situations without paralyzing my Coachees. I simply ask them:

- "Tell me about a situation that tends to bring out your worst, that turns you into that person that you don't want to be, but are anyway."—see Appendix.

Like the values request, the Coachees will spend a few minutes thinking about a situation, and then tell me the story. Most often, that story will tie itself back to a personal value that they had listed when they described themselves to me. Every so often though, the offended value isn't present. In most cases, it's because we're only working with three or four words, rather than six, eight, or ten. So we proceed to identify it together, and then add it. That sounds something like:

- "Thank you for sharing that story with me."
- "I'm not sure I see a personal value on the list that you created earlier that might have been offended by that particular behavior."
- "What personal value of yours do you feel might have been offended in that case?"
- "Do I have your permission to add it to your list?"

In a perfect world, we would take the time to work through each and every one of their hot situations, and identify which offended personal value is spinning them up. However, due to time constraints, I usually ask them to record the situations (as they occur) in a journal. That gives us ample substance for future coaching sessions.

I would ask that you (the reader), do the same.

- Please find a comfortable way (for you) to document the situations that turn you into that person that you don't want to be, but are anyway.

When you analyze those situations dispassionately, you'll come to realize that those situations were "hot" due to the emotional load that you put on them, as a result of one of your personal values being offended. By the end of this book, you'll learn how to free yourself of the control those situations once had on you.

STEP TWO–IDENTIFYING HOT SITUATIONS

"What matters most is how well you walk through the fire."
—Charles Bukowski

Hot Situations and Offended Values—I

"Marty, I'd like you to tell me about a situation that tends to bring out your worst. That turns you into that person that you don't want to be, but are anyway." I said. "Take a moment, envision the situation, and write it down for me."

Marty took a few minutes, and once completed, I asked him to share his scenario.

"It's usually when I'm under pressure," he said. "Like, when I have a couple of guys standing at the counter, and the phone is ringing."

"How often does that happen?"

"It happens a lot," he said. "There are only two of us in the department and when Phil is off, I work alone. I cover the retail counter, the wholesale counter, and the phones. Some days it's overwhelming. It's worst when one of the guys at the counter needs something I don't have."

"Why is that worst?"

"Because when they learn I don't have it, there's always a nasty comment that follows," he explained.

"What sort of comment?"

"Usually it's something like, 'I think we should have that,'" he said.

"Okay, and then what happens?"

Before answering, his look indicated that he thought I was a little thick. "That's when the argument starts," he said, like it was the only imaginable outcome.

"And how does the argument start?"

"Well, when they say: 'I think we should have that,' they mean: 'YOU DON'T KNOW HOW TO DO YOUR JOB!' AND NOTHING INFURIATES ME MORE THAN SOMEONE QUESTIONING MY ABILITY TO DO MY JOB...ESPECIALLY SOMEONE WHO DOESN'T EVEN KNOW WHAT MY JOB IS! I KNOW HOW TO DO MY JOB!"

I let the words hang for a moment, and let the energy clear, remaining silent.

After the outburst, Marty calmed down a bit and said, "Sorry... just thinking about that gets me wound up," he admitted.

"Marty," I began, "did Jim (the technician) say the words, 'You don't know how to do your job?'"

"Well no, he didn't say those words... but that's what he meant."

"Okay, but what did he say again?"

"He said, 'I think we should have that,'" he affirmed.

"So, how did you get from him saying, 'I think we should have that' to you hearing, 'You don't know how to do your job?'"

"Because, I'm always overhearing chatter around the building about running out of stuff and how they believe it's my fault."

"Like they believe you do it intentionally?" I asked.

"Yes, they believe I do it on purpose."

"And do you?"

"No, of course not. You can't have every part under the sun, there isn't enough space to stock it all, and the carrying costs are too high. So I do my best to have the high-travel parts available all the time. The technicians don't know, or care, about the difference though. They think whatever part they need is one I should have."

"Marty, earlier we talked about personal values, and how those personal values manifest in people's behavior, and that—"

"All human behavior is a function of personal values," he said, finishing my sentence.

"Yes, exactly," I said. "And conflict exists—"

"When someone feels like one of their personal values is offended," he said, again finishing my sentence.

"How was I participating in the problem?" he asked indignantly.

"Meeting conflict with conflict," I said. "How often do you argue with yourself?"

"If I did that, they'd be questioning my sanity," he said.

"That's the point," I said. "People don't argue with themselves, it requires another willing participant. In your case, it was with Jim. In Jim's case, it was with you. If either of you didn't participate, there couldn't have been an argument. Jim experienced a situation that challenged one of his personal values: the Parts Department didn't have a part available that he needed to complete a job. Given that offense, he emotionally reacted by lashing out, and challenged the fact that the part wasn't available. That situation became a trigger for you by you interpreting his comment to indict your ability to do your job, and in turn, you reacted to his reaction, making the situation worse, not better. How well do you know Jim?"

"I know him pretty well," Marty said. "We've worked together a long time."

"Marty, I'm curious . . . do you feel like Jim could relate to the personal values you identified earlier: timeliness/promptness, dependability, work ethic, commitment, honesty, trustworthiness, and competence?"

"I'm sure he does," Marty declared. "He's one of the top producers . . . always has been."

"Which personal values specifically, Marty?"

"Definitely competence, work ethic, commitment, and dependability. Probably all of them to a degree."

"If that's true, Marty, you both share some personal values. How do you generally react to a situation where you need something to complete a task, but find that what you need isn't available?"

"Of course, I don't like it. It slows me down and holds things up."

"Which of your personal values does that interfere with, Marty?"

"Probably all of them, in a certain way."

"Could that be true for Jim, as well?"

"Yeah, I think it could. I can see how that would bother him from a responsibility point of view. People depend on him to get a job done and he wants to deliver on that."

"Okay, great work, Marty . . . good insight. Can you imagine, that when Jim learned that your department didn't have what he needed to complete the job he was doing, his reply evidenced that he was simply reacting to one of his personal values being offended, which led to you defending yours?"

"Yes, I can see that now. Man, it's always easier when you're not in the moment; you know what I mean?"

"The biggest irony, to me, is that you were both defending personal values. You both want to get a job done. You both want to be seen as competent, dependable, trustworthy, and committed. I'd like you to put yourself back in that moment now. Think about how the situation unfolded. Think about the way that you emotionally reacted. Let me know when you feel like you're back in that moment."

"Okay."

"Now, try to imagine a different response . . . a response that wouldn't result in an argument."

"I guess I could have said: 'You know Jim, you might be right. Maybe we should have that part. Let's check to see how often we've needed that item in the last few months. If we've needed it more than I think we have, we'll stock it going forward. I'm sorry I don't have it for you now, but I'll get it for you as soon as I can.'"

"Perfect! Does the situation feel different to you now?"

"It feels less charged, less confrontational, less about me."

"That's great work, good job. How confident are you that you'll be able to respond that way in the future, in a real situation?"

"It's going to take some work, but I think that working through it like this will help me get ahead of it next time."

"Great, that's real progress. You should be proud of that new perspective.

I know we've spent some time on this, Marty, and you've made some real progress," I prepped. "I'd like to continue, though. The only way to successfully manage emotional reactions is by first identifying the situations that cause them. When you do that, they lose their control over you. We won't have enough time to identify every one of them today, but I'd like to hear at least one more," I instructed. "Are there any other situations, circumstances, interactions, or individuals that bring out your worst?"

"There is a woman in another department, her name is Dawn," Marty began. "Just the sight of her raises the hair on the back of my neck."

"Wait a minute," I interrupted. "Are you saying that you get a physical reaction when anticipating your interaction with her?"

"Yes, that's right," he confessed.

"Wow," I said, surprised by the nature of Marty's physical reaction. "How do those conversations go?"

His expression didn't require words. It clearly communicated, *Do you really need to ask?*

"What's beneath that physical reaction, Marty? What's driving that?" I asked, hoping he could pinpoint it.

"SHE ALWAYS SHOWS UP UNPREPARED!" he explained. "SHE NEVER HAS THE INFORMATION I NEED TO HELP HER PROCESS THE ORDERS SHE WANTS TO PROCESS! I'VE GIVEN PRICE SHEETS TO HER DEPARTMENT MANAGER, BUT SHE IS CONSTANTLY ASKING ME FOR PRICES! I JUST DON'T THINK SHE GIVES A SHIT!"

Again, it was obvious that this was a hot situation for Marty. So after the storm, I asked, "What is it, specifically with respect to her behavior, that has become a trigger for you, Marty?"

"I don't know, it just bothers me," he stated. "I know I couldn't go through the day behaving like she does, I'd lose my job."

"So, are we talking about fairness?" I searched.

"Yeah, I guess that could be some of it," he agreed.

"Do you feel it's unfair for her to behave the way she does, like she's getting away with something, or is it more to do with how able and committed she is to her job?"

"I think she should be better at her job," he answered almost immediately.

"And which of your values is being expressed now?"

"That must be competence."

"Do you think competence is one of Dawn's values?"

"Probably not," Marty said, "or she does a real good job hiding it."

"Well if not competence, Marty, what do you suppose she values?" I asked.

"She's really good with customers and relationships . . . people really like her," he said. "She always has customers coming in bringing her gifts; cookies, flowers, coffee, etc.," he finished.

"Okay, so maybe her values include warmth, empathy, trust, communication, and service, those types of things," I speculated. "Marty, is it possible that you may be judging Dawn based on your own personal values? Maybe projecting what is important to you onto her, and then being disappointed when it doesn't translate to her behavior?"

"I guess I could be doing some of that," he acknowledged.

"If Dawn wasn't truly good at her job, if she wasn't competent, do you think she could successfully build and maintain customer relationships the way she does?"

"Probably not."

"Marty, could it be true that Dawn is competent, but measures that competence by her customer's feelings and actions, rather than measuring herself with respect to memorizing your department's price sheet?"

"I can see how that could be true." "When Dawn comes back to your department, asking you for prices, is it usually for herself or for her customers?" I inquired.

"Always customers," he said. "And it's usually in response to one of their phone calls."

"Knowing how committed Dawn is to her customers and those relationships, Marty, could you imagine a way to partner with Dawn, so that you could have more confidence in her pricing knowledge and she could more quickly and easily serve her customers?"

"I guess I could spend some time working with her one-on-one."

"That's a great idea, Marty. And what about the hair on the back of your neck now?" I teased.

"It seems like it doesn't bother me the same way anymore."

"Great, that's what we're after," I celebrated. "Good job, Marty. You've come a long way in a few short hours." Indeed, he had.

Hot Situations and Offended Values—II

"David, I have another question I'd like to ask you. Much like when I asked you to describe yourself to a stranger earlier," I said, "I'd like you to tell me about a situation that tends to bring out your worst; one that turns you into that person that you don't want to be, but are anyway."

"I've already touched on it a number of times," he said. "It's when my people don't perform to the level that I know they're capable of."

"I know you already run one of the most efficient operations around, David—based on what I see elsewhere."

"That might be true, but we can do better. But they have to want it," he said, referring to his people's motivation level. "And they just don't. And I don't understand it. I'll never understand it."

"David, we have some direct employee feedback from the survey. The most common and collective response from the employees as a group is that they all feel a little overworked. How do you square their response with your feelings that they aren't driven enough?"

"I have no idea," he replied, flabbergasted. "There are only so many hours in a day to be productive. We're in a fortunate position, because business has been good, to be able to offer everyone additional work if they want it. But no one seems to want it. They talk more about being home with their families than they do about making a living . . . I just don't get it! And I've tried, believe me I've tried. I just can't seem to get my point across, to help them understand how important it is to be as productive as they can be. Pushing doesn't work . . . I don't know. I'm not sure what the next move is," he said, sounding a little resigned.

"How well do you know your people?" I asked.

"I know them. I mean, I work with them, you know. If you're asking whether I know what they like to do in their off time, or their kids names, stuff like that . . . I don't really know that stuff. I've always been reluctant to get too close to the people I work with."

"David, let's go back to the concept of time for a moment. If you had only one hour to spend doing something, would you spend it working or doing something else?"

"I'd probably spend it working," he said. "I'm not proud of that, but it's true. It's probably also what's behind the stuff going on at home too."

"David," I asked, "how do you think your people would respond to that question?"

"I think they would all choose to do something else."

"What do you think they would do? How would they spend that hour differently?"

"I'm sure they would all do something with their families, their children," he explained.

"So for them, you believe an incremental hour with their families is worth more than an incremental hour of work," I clarified. "For you though, it's different. The incremental hour of work is more valuable. Do you feel like your people associate a cost with respect to being away from their families?"

"I'm sure they do, but they have to make a living."

"Do you associate a cost with respect to being away from your family?" I asked, acknowledging the sensitive nature of the question.

"Not really . . . I've always put my job first, ahead of my family," he said, in a somewhat detached manner.

"Is it possible, David, that your willingness to prioritize work over family—based on you expressing and protecting your values of work ethic, time, and money—is simply clashing with your people's unwillingness to do the same, based on their expressing and protecting their value of family?"

"I never thought about it like that, but I guess that would explain a lot," he recognized.

"One of the best reasons to get to know your people a little better, David, is it will help you understand what drives them," I explained. "It may be the case that they are as driven as you are, but in a different way. If you both learn to respect and appreciate each other's personal values and different perspectives, you may find that together you can accomplish more. It may help you break through that performance wall you talked about. But first, you may need to recognize that sometimes we, ourselves, are responsible for creating the behavior in others that we don't want. When we impose our personal values on others, and we measure them based on how well we believe they are honoring those values, that's a recipe for disappointment. Conflict exists, not only when someone feels like one of their personal values has been offended, but also if one feels like another is imposing their personal values on them. And if true, it would be natural for them to react. If they react in conflict, then they will push back. And the harder you push, the harder they'll push back. And that's how the situation becomes so unmanageable for everyone. Tragically, you end up pushing against yourself to the point of exhaustion and sheer befuddlement. Does any of that sound familiar?"

"Wow . . . like you've been following me around," he said. "Like you've been following me around . . ."

REACTION: THE CREATION OF EMOTIONAL ENERGY

"Your problem isn't the problem. Your reaction is the problem."
—Anonymous

I t begins in the pit of your stomach—boooooooom! You saw something. You heard something. You felt something. The impulse travels at the speed of light from your brain to that point in your gut. In something like two billionths of a second, the message is encoded, transmitted, and decoded. The instructions lead to your heart quickening, your muscles tightening, your body tensing, a state of readiness . . .

That minuscule explosion on a cellular level mimics the cosmic scale of a stellar explosion, when a star turns into a supernova. There is a moment, when the force of gravity—that irresistible force—has exerted such pressure, for so long, that it results in the collapse of the star. At that point, a vast amount of energy is released, which spreads at speeds exploring galactic limits, for periods of time measured in human lifespans.

Gravity in the cosmic sense is no different than personal values in the human sense. Gravity is ubiquitous, ever-vigilant, pervasive, and limitless. There is no waking up one day and contemplating choices based on the absence of gravity. It *is*.

Likewise, personal values *are*. If one of your personal values is honesty, for example, it won't occur every other Tuesday at 10:00 a.m. Or every second Saturday. Or when it's sunny and warm. Or when vacationing in Alaska. If honesty is a personal value, you will *always* behave honestly, and you will expect the same of others. That isn't to say that you'll always tell someone their baby's ugly, but being honest is your default setting. Faced with truth being unnecessarily destructive though, you might intentionally mitigate the potential harm that it might cause by blending your personal value of honesty with some other of your personal values; kindness, for example. You modify the message in a way that still meets the rigor of truthfulness, but softened in delivery. Honesty and kindness then become a hybrid way that you measure yourself and everyone else.

In prior chapters, we discussed personal values at length: how to identify them, and learning that conflict exists when one feels like one of their personal values has been offended or when one feels like another is imposing their personal values on them. Next, we learned that certain situations are prone to offending those personal values, and in order to manage those hot situations, one must first identify them. This chapter is dedicated to reactions: the causes, the results, and their character.

Reactions come in a couple of different flavors. A behavioral psychologist or neuroscientist might talk about reactions in terms of a person's autonomic nervous system, sympathetic nervous system, and parasympathetic nervous system, working in unison to collectively manage and regulate the body's physiological response and recovery to any threatening stimulus. That aside, you're probably more familiar with the more generic characterization termed *fight or flight*. Fight or flight—coined by Walter Bradford Cannon, professor and chairman of the Department of Physiology at Harvard Medical School, in 1915—has achieved inclusion in our modern popular lexicon. Cannon first introduced the concept in his work *Bodily Changes in Pain, Hunger, Fear and Rage: An Account of Recent Researches into the Function of Emotional Excitement.*

Since Cannon's initial work over one hundred years ago, there has been some disagreement, in a chicken-or-egg kind of way, challenging the idea of which comes first: emotions leading to physiological changes in the body, or physiological changes in the body leading to emotions. For us, though, it's neither worth the time nor effort to delve in to the argument, for it makes no difference which comes first with respect to conflict. What *is* useful to know, is that *both* emotions and physiological changes play a part in fight or flight and conflict.

For the sake of eliminating any confusion going forward, I'm going to rephrase fight or flight in to more appropriate coaching terms. As such, fight becomes a reaction in conflict, and flight becomes a victim's reaction. We covered the energetic levels of Victim and Conflict in the Readiness chapter.

It begins in the pit of your stomach—booooooom! You saw something. You heard something. You felt something. The impulse travels at the speed of light from your brain to that point in your gut. In something like two billionths of a second, the message is encoded, transmitted, and decoded. Those instructions lead to your heart quickening, your muscles tightening, your body tensing, and you in a state of readiness. Simultaneously, a cascade of emotions floods the consciousness: fear, agitation, anger, dread, and stress. The senses are on fire, acutely monitoring everything via exceptionally heightened awareness. Those emotional and physiological changes produce the energy necessary for one to *act*. With respect to conflict, it is the energy necessary for one to *react*.

What has led to such a cataclysmic energetic acceleration? A personal value was offended.

- Conflict exists when someone feels like one of their personal values has been offended.

The offense can occur by simply witnessing another's behavior that is not in keeping with one's own personal values, or if one's personal values are called into question by another. Using the prior reference to honesty, for instance, if one's honesty is directly challenged, or one witnesses another being dishonest, their personal value of honesty will be offended.

When the personal value is offended, in the metaphorical celestial sense, that is the moment when gravity crushes the star's core, beginning a catastrophic reaction destroying the astral body itself. Boooooooom! In interpersonal terms, the moment a personal value is offended, a reaction immediately follows. Depending on one's default style of reaction, that reaction will be as a Victim or in Conflict. A Victim, withdraws, stops communicating, feels helpless and powerless, and thinks, *I lose*. In Conflict, one lashes out, becomes angry and aggressive, argumentative and combative, and thinks, *I win*. Both reactions are negative. Both create winners and losers, and when the winner wins, it's directly at the loser's expense. We are not our best selves, nor do we produce the best outcomes, when we are reactive. Complicating the intensity of the reaction, an emotional hijacking can occur, shutting down the problem-solving part of our brains. This prepares us for confrontation, but conspires against our ability to think our way out of it.

In iPEC coaching terms, one reactionary style is "less worse" than the other, primarily because one style is more likely than the other to preserve one's existence. And that that style, Conflict energy, is one step above, and closer, to the first positive energetic level, Responsibility. The inherent shortcoming in reacting as a Victim is that one will not rise up to defend oneself. That reaction is mired in blame, rationalization, apathy, and lethargy. For me personally, working with the Victim reaction is the most difficult and challenging. I rebel most strongly against the idea of being limited, controlled, or defenseless. Had I reacted as a Victim during my childhood, I wouldn't have survived. Given that style's foreign nature, I often employ The Arbinger Institute's *The Anatomy of Peace*. It has become my favorite resource for working with the Victim reaction.

In that book, they tell a story of a frightened young woman running away after being dropped off by her parents at a place for her restoration, but she had no previous idea she would be going there. Upon learning she would be spending several weeks living off the land while summoning the demons that had been complicating her life thus far, she fled. And she was barefoot. Running in one-hundred-degree heat, the pavement burned her feet with every step. The Institute's staff pursued her in a way that let her know they were close enough to render aid if she wanted it, but not close enough to ever be threatening. They also took off their own shoes to suffer along with her, to let her know they were willing to feel the pain along with her. Doing so, they invited peace in her heart, when until then her heart was at war.

Unlike the Victim reaction, I need no other resource for assistance when working with Conflict. It was who I was for so long, that it's like navigating a lifelong residence with eyes closed. Recognizing each and every creak, groan, and squeak, as a clue to one's exact location, accommodating the sightless and effortless maneuver.

Reacting in Conflict occurs as a result of one feeling that one of their personal values has been offended. It's immaterial what that value actually is, all values offense's act equally and identically. Booooooom! The offense creates emotion within the offended party. The emotion is the energy to act, or in the case of Conflict, react. The offended party feels incredulous that another is acting in opposition to their value. Case in point, if the value were trustworthiness, the other person might be behaving in an untrustworthy way. Or the other person might have challenged the trustworthiness of the offended party. Likewise, if the value were dependability, determination, amicableness, sincerity, considerateness, competitiveness . . . whatever. It doesn't matter. The reactive energy is fuel to prompt the action necessary to counter the offense. It is the energy to argue one's position, to advocate for the conviction of the offending party, to confront the offensive behavior, to physically intervene on one's behalf, or to right the *perceived* wrong. The offended party's incredulity is spurred on by the inability to conceive of living in a world that is absent their offended value. That value then becomes synonymous with their identity. It's no longer *I behave honestly*; it is, *I am honest*. So when someone challenges that value, or behaves in opposition to that value, for the opposed party, the earth shakes. The opposing behavior is challenging *who they are.*

No human being wants to inhabit a world in which who they are is being continuously challenged, feeling the need for the constant defense and justification in an effort to counter another's *perceived* prejudicial attack. That's why an offended value can lead to such acrimony. It's a *perceived* indictment of one's very existence.

It's no different when someone feels they are being judged with respect to someone else's values.

- Conflict exists when someone feels like another is imposing their personal values on them.

Meaning that, if for one, respect is a personal value, that person will measure all others based on their own interpretation of those others honoring that value. The personal value holder will become anxious and frustrated—emotionally reactive—if the others' behavior is not in keeping with *that* personal value. This is the essence of imposing personal values on others. The belief, and reliance on that belief, that only one set of personal values exists in the world—*one's own*. That is precisely why heightened self-awareness, and the elevated awareness of others, is so necessary. It frees oneself from the self-imposed prison that Conflict puts us in.

I'm often asked to work with co-workers, especially those working together closely and who are creating the behaviors in each other that they each don't want. It's simply a compound situation, where each person is reacting to the other. It can become like tennis, back and forth, to and fro, a reactive volley, stuck in a continuous loop.

When that is true, I begin the work with one of the individuals first. I run them through my five-step process beginning by:

- Asking them to describe themselves to a stranger;
- Followed by asking them for a situation that tends to bring out their worst—it often includes the second individual—
- We then explore their default reactionary style;
- We discuss the cognitive concepts that lead to interrupting that reaction;

- And we transform the negative emotional reaction into a positive response, one they can be proud of.

Then I repeat work with the second individual.

Once complete, I get them together and work with them both. The idea in working with them individually is to heighten their own self-awareness. When together, it's to elevate the awareness of each other.

When we begin the work together, the first thing we do is compare words—the personal values that each has declared. Usually, if each has given me eight to ten words, one or two of the words might be the same, but often the words vary widely. So, after setting up the discussion by reviewing both sets of words side-by-side, I'll say to one of them: "Hey, I noticed that your words are not the same as your colleague's." And then I'll ask: "So, which one of your colleague's words is bad or wrong?" That question usually strikes terror in them, and is always met with hesitation—keep in mind they are doing this in front of each other. But after the momentary freeze, the answer comes. "Ah, none of them are bad or wrong, they're their words."

"Well," I'll say, "they're not the same as yours, so they must be bad or wrong." At some point, they'll understand I'm baiting them. Then they usually respond with zest. They become energized by the conversation and the opportunity to make their point. In tennis terms, they employ the overhead smash. The conversation usually goes like this:

"No," they say, "none of them are bad or wrong. I have my words, and they have their words. I'm entitled to my words, and they're entitled to their words. We all have our words."

"Okay," I'll reply. "So, if they are not bad or wrong, what are they then?"

"What do you mean?"

"I mean, they're not the same as yours, but they're not bad or wrong, so what are they then . . . in comparison to yours?"

Right around now, they are experiencing mild displeasure, a little annoyed that I don't get it. "What are they?" I'll repeat. It usually takes a moment, a little uncomfortable silence, a little awkwardness, a few glances of puzzlement. Then the circuit completes, the connection is made. "Different," they say.

As we work through the process, I'll remind them of the fundamental principles:

- All Human behavior is a function of personal values.
- Conflict exists when someone feels like one of their personal values has been offended, or if someone feels like another is imposing their personal values on them.
- Certain situations will tend to offend one's personal values; in order to manage those hot situations, one must first be able to identify them.
- When one's personal values are offended, one will spin-up emotionally.
- The resulting emotion must be suppressed or expressed.
- If suppressed, the reaction will be as a victim.
- If expressed, the reaction will be in conflict.

We'll revisit the situations they each said tended to bring out their worst. We'll try to understand which personal value was offended by the behavior they witnessed in the situation they described. Helping them pinpoint which personal value was offended also helps them understand why the behavior they witnessed felt so offensive. Helping them understand that that perceived offensiveness is what led to them emotionally loading the situation.

RAMPAGE: BEING CONFLICT, AND HIGHLY REACTIVE

*"So go ahead, break stuff. Break yourself on
the once-hard edges of yourself.
And recycle the debris into the foundation of your future."*
—Mark Twight

Being Conflict

When situations become emotionally loaded, bad things happen. I was the king of emotionally loading situations. The thing that made those situations worst—mostly for whoever was opposite me—was my lack of understanding and practice of the concept of proportionality. I'm sure your familiar with the saying: "Don't bring a knife to a gunfight." If I were in that gunfight, metaphorically, I'd bring an atomic bomb. I unleashed it *all,* and *at once.* Looking back, I'd say I never only reacted . . . I overreacted every time. Why? I perceived each offense to be about who I was. It became another reason I wasn't good enough. So, for any person who has an average ability to manage conflict with a reactive intensity of five on a scale of ten, mine was a twelve or fifteen. When I reacted, I was releasing decades of resentment, stores of rage, and a ferocious protest against the unfairness of life. That tremendous energy would be concentrated, focused, and aimed at whoever happened to offend *my value*. Shock and awe. Like going fishing with dynamite.

I didn't realize it then, but I had simply become a puppet. I allowed myself to be ruled by my emotions and had no ability to self-manage. I felt like people were pushing my buttons—what I now know to be offending my personal values—all day, every day. I lived chronically spun-up. In reality, I had surrendered my control to those around me, allowing them to control my behavior by virtue of the personal value they offended. Aggravated by what I now believe to be post-traumatic stress disorder of abandonment, stuck in a kind of obsessive hypervigilance, eternally defensive, to the point that my defensiveness *became offensive to others*. That was the cruelest irony, epitomized by the complete absence of self-awareness, an epic blind-spot—one that led to me creating the behavior in others that I didn't want.

I've always felt that my primary role was to provide. Provide for myself, my wife, my son, for our lives. Since the day that my stepfather grabbed me by the ear, taking me to the local restaurant for a job, work was the way I provided for myself. It was my freedom. I've always had a high capacity to work. My motto was, "work longer and harder than the next guy." The Army instilled an even greater work ethic in me. When I got out, I worked what seemed like half days, twelve hours. I worked landscaping during the day, picked orders for a natural food distributor second shift, and loaded trucks until midnight. The work was physically demanding, and it came to be just a day's pay for a day's work, not really a vocation or career, just a temporary way to make a living.

I answered an ad for a job selling cars. I started selling cars and making more money. By the second year, I out-earned my mother and my stepfather combined. I worked bell-to-bell—essentially every hour the dealership was open. In those days, after work there would be a stampede to the local bar. The dealership would close at 9:00 p.m. and the bar would close at 2:00 a.m. It wasn't uncommon to close both, and be back at work at 7:00 a.m. Drinking was part of it, and by then I had become a professional. It never got in the way of work. I learned that in the Army.

While stationed at Fort Polk, we had weekends off. Usually, we would head off to Lake Charles, Houston, Galveston, Corpus Christi, Baton Rouge, Shreveport, or New Orleans. The pattern was always the same. We'd hit some bar, get hammered, start or finish a brawl, and then report back to work. I perfected running PT (physical training) and vomiting at the same time. The drinking was a way of life. I never thought about it as a problem; it was one, of course, but I didn't see it . . . another epic blindspot. It probably should have been blindingly obvious; there were signs, and the signs weren't subtle. Many times, I would wake up on the sidewalk outside a bar with no idea how I got there. I remember one morning, waking up in the bed of a pick-up truck. It was daylight, but early. A couple of girls were walking by and saw me in the bed of the truck. They took one look at me and said, "Wow . . . man, you look like shit." Looking in the mirror, I could see what they were talking about; my face was a bloody mess. My eye was split open, and the blood had dried all over my face. It wasn't that painful, but it looked worse. I vaguely remember getting hit by something the night before, but the alcohol had acted as an anesthetic. None of that mattered to me though. I needed to get stitched up, cleaned up, and back to work. It was just another weekend.

This, and the next several years, were the most dangerous period of my life. I had nothing to lose. It didn't matter to me if I woke up those mornings or not. "The good die young," I thought, and I was anxious to prove that. The *only* mechanism I possessed, with respect to keeping my composure, disappeared after the first kamikaze or Absolut on the rocks. The rage itself was problem enough, but couple that with the loss of restraint and cognitive impairment that comes along with drinking, and the result is a superheated, hair-triggered, chain reaction blast, ready to blow at the slightest provocation . . . which was often someone bumping in to me in a bar.

I had enlisted in the Army with the intent on becoming a Green Beret, the Army's elite special forces group. When, I took the ASVAB—Armed Services Vocational Aptitude Battery—my recruiter asked me how I thought I did. I remember telling him I thought it was easy, and I remember the look on his face. "Sure it was, kid." Turns out, I maxed it. So that meant I could choose any job in the Army. I took the DLAT—Defense Language Aptitude Test—too, and maxed that as well. They offered me an accounting job at Fort Benjamin Harrison in Indiana, or a year at UCLA, the Defense Language Institute, learning languages. I asked the recruiter which job would get me to SF (Special Forces), and he said I would have to join the Infantry. He said that, while in boot camp, I would have an opportunity to volunteer for Jump School—Army Airborne Parachute Training—after which, I could volunteer for Ranger School—Army Combat Leadership Course-Small Unit Tactics—and if I made it through all that, I might have a shot at SF. Without hesitation, I asked him to sign me up. In the military, we have a saying, "No battle plan survives the first shot fired." Mike Tyson is famous for saying, "Everyone has a plan until they're punched in the mouth." My military career was a little like that. In boot camp, due to an Army experiment—Cohort Platoons, where the entire unit is trained together, and then shipped to the same duty station—we weren't able to volunteer for Jump School or Ranger School. When we got our orders upon graduation, we were all going to Fort Polk, LA—the Mechanized Infantry.

When I got to my duty station, my company commander told

me I was going to West Point, via the United States Military Academy Preparatory School at Fort Monmouth, New Jersey. My GT (General Technical Score) was near the highest in the battalion. He said they would process my paperwork to get me in for the upcoming year, and not to get too comfortable. In the meantime, I would drive for him and handle some miscellaneous duties. Of which, they sent me to the AUSA (Association of the United States Army) Conference in Washington, D.C., to represent my unit. My package to West Point Prep didn't make the deadline, so my company commander said that I wouldn't be going that year, but would go next year. Again he said, "Don't get comfortable." Ultimately, when my package got processed, I didn't get accepted.

It didn't shock me. I was a terrible student, and I hardly went to high school the year it mattered most. I was too busy working. I never stayed back; I could do the work. I put up A's in summer school, but I couldn't have cared less about applying myself and getting good grades. After being turned down to West Point Prep, I was recycled back into my regular unit for the remainder of my enlistment. Just prior to my ETS (End Term of Service), I was offered Special Forces Medic training. A little disillusioned by that point, I decided not to reenlist and to take a shot in the private sector. I had served honorably. I earned two Army Commendation Medals, five Army Achievement Medals, an Expert Infantry Badge, was recognized as Soldier of the Month, and was on the promotion to Non-Commissioned Officer list in under three years. Had I not saved up my leave to shorten my enlistment, I would have earned a Good Conduct Medal. I served just short of three years, needing a full three years to earn the distinction.

It probably shouldn't come as any surprise to learn that I met my wife in a bar. More accurately, I should say re-met. One year, we were in the same Spanish class in high school. After a long week, I was trying to get a drink. The place was packed, and the bartender was ignoring me. Immediately agitated by that, I began waving a hundred-dollar bill in the air to get his attention. Over the din I heard her say, "I can help you with that."

"Great," I said. "I appreciate it."

"Jimmy," she called, "I need a drink."

We talked for a bit, and we made a date to go to the beach the next day. It was Memorial Day weekend. Within three months, we were engaged and, in less than a year, married. My wife's father had been battling cancer, and he wanted to see his daughter married before he died. He was forty-six years old when he died, and we held his hand when he took his last breath. Between that drink and getting married, there were many times that I was completely out of control. I had a tendency to be an instant asshole—just add alcohol. It got to a point where she insisted that if I continued drinking, she was leaving. It was an ultimatum, drinking or her, and that demand saved my life.

Work became the new addiction, and I worked as hard as I drank—as long too. The long hours in the car business were always a challenge. I viewed my time spent working as fulfilling my obligation to provide. Providing was one of my values. And because my father had never provided for me, there was no force on earth that was going to stop me from providing for my family. Only death would stop me.

I climbed the ladder pretty quickly. I went from selling cars, to finance and insurance manager, to sales manager, to general sales manager by the time I was twenty-five. The dealership's owner had three children in the business and owned seven other locations. His oldest son was the chief executive officer. That son was trying to buy one of the dealerships from his father. He offered me a buy-in, ten percent for seventy-five thousand dollars. We would transition the business entirely over fifteen years. Me earning in, him earning out. I took a mortgage out on a relative's house, along with pledging my own house as additional collateral to raise the money. With money in hand, I was ready to do the deal. Shortly before the deal closed, the Rhode Island Share and Deposit Indemnity Corporation (RISDIC), the insurer of the State's non-FDIC (Federal Deposit Insurance Corporation) credit unions, was found to be insolvent.

On January 1st, 1991, the governor ordered all non-FDIC and non-NCUA (National Credit Union Administration) credit unions to be closed immediately, indefinitely. All of the dealership group's operating accounts were in one of those closed credit unions. The group filed Chapter 11 bankruptcy shortly afterwards. It was later converted to Chapter 7, liquidating all remaining assets. I hung in until the end. I ran my part of the dealership during the bankruptcy under the direction of a bank trustee. We couldn't put gas in a car without that person's permission. Earlier that year, the CEO was negotiating to buy a dealership group in New Hampshire. He had been pricing the purchase of two Bell Jet Ranger Helicopters to shuttle back and forth between the Rhode Island and New Hampshire locations. He was driving a Lotus Esprit Turbo, which he occasionally let me take for a weekend. When we had a good month, our reward would be a weekend at his condo on Loon Mountain in New Hampshire. It was a work-hard, play-hard culture. That changed in the blink of an eye. I was the last of four hundred employees.

Beyond the dealership group's struggles, the CEO had recently opened the first ecologically friendly body shop, outfitted with the latest and greatest green technology: fresh air systems for the paint crew, recycled water and filtration systems, water-based paints and solvents, and special remediation equipment for any hazardous waste. It was twenty-five thousand feet of hospital-clean space, producing assembly-line-like productivity with military precision.

It was well-fed when the dealerships were in full operation. After the bankruptcy filing though, that changed. The body shop was in danger of closing as well. One day, I was talking with the owner, my prospective partner in the dealership.

"I can't make rent," he said.

"How much?" I asked him.

"Twenty-five thousand."

"I have the money," I said. "I can help you with that. I know you'll pay me back."

So, I put up the twenty-five thousand. That bought him another month of operation. In the end, it only made a small difference. The body shop closed, and I got partially paid back a couple years later, in cars.

Losing my job, and twenty-five grand, didn't help matters. I still had the new mortgage to pay for, with the additional pressure of it being on my relative's house. I bounced around to some other dealerships, but it wasn't the same. I just couldn't find my place.

It was around this time—it might have been Christmas, New Year, or in February, my birthday curse as I've come to call it—that we had a few people over to our condo. Among the guests were my neighbor and his wife, my prospective partner and his date, and a few of our former high school friends. It was getting late, many of the people had already left, and my neighbor made some comment about me "thinking I knew everything" to the remaining guests. We had all been drinking all night, and what could have been laughed off wasn't. I was already on edge with my neighbor after my wife told me that he had come into our condo one day, unannounced and uninvited. She was just getting out of the shower, and there he was.

As soon as I heard those words, I told him to get the fuck out of my house. Like mice scurrying away from a lurking cat, everyone scattered. Once everyone was gone, in a moment of unusual self-doubt, I thought maybe I could have handled that better. I thought I should probably go apologize to the neighbor, so I went next door and rang the bell. I never saw the punch coming, but it came as the door opened. And then the door closed again. I never got a chance to apologize, and after getting hit, I became "that guy." I remember trying to kick the door in, which is when someone called the police.

The police showed up asking who owned the house. My wife kept telling them she did, but they didn't believe her. She was only in her early twenties then. They must have thought it was her father's place. I think I told them I owned the fucking house, just to put a fine point on it. They said they had received a complaint from a neighbor, and were responding to a disturbance. In my view they were just making a bad situation worse, so I remained combative. They threatened to arrest me, and I told them I didn't give a fuck if they arrested me or not. Unsurprisingly, they handcuffed me, transported me to the local police department, processed me, and put me in a holding cell for several hours to think about it. I met with the chief as I was getting released, who had received a call on my behalf from a family friend and a former police officer himself. The chief explained how to handle the hearing, the charge of disturbing the peace, and how after a year I could get it expunged, which I did.

Also around this time, my stepfather died of mesothelioma, leaving my mother alone. He and I were never that close, but he was good to my mother. He had a special patience and tolerance for her mental illness; one I never had, because I selfishly wanted a "normal" mother, and life. I remember when I was young, one of the times my mother was in treatment, he beat the shit out of me because I told a friend my mother was crazy. My mother received a number of settlements after he died, his death a result of exposure to asbestos, the exposure coming during the time he worked at the shipyard at Quonset Point, Rhode Island. My mother had always been a wizard with money, seemingly able to produce a dollar twenty-five out of every dollar. When I turned sixteen, she took me to the bank and had me take a passbook loan on some of the money I had saved. She helped me get my credit established, which led to me being able to buy my first house at twenty-three years old.

I made a deal with her to borrow some money to capitalize a business. I would pay her back with a higher rate of interest, which would increase her cash flow on a monthly basis. It was good for her and good for me. I opened a used car sales and service business in January, 1994, after having spent several months getting through the licensing process, hanging signs, installing equipment, and populating the initial inventory. We did over $100,000 in sales our first full month. I had spent years learning how to operate a new car dealership, so I just set up my used car business the same way. The only difference was that I had to learn the service business this time.

The moment I learned that you keep seven cents on a dollar when you sell cars, and seventy cents on a dollar when you fix them, I fell in love with the service business. Every waking hour thereafter, I was thinking about how to grow the service business. We tested many different promotions, but after taking a macroeconomics class, introducing me to supply and demand and price elasticity of demand, I had an idea to promote a loss leader air-conditioning campaign. We offered to service air-conditioning systems for $49.95, including refilling the system with up to two pounds of refrigerant. Refrigerant (R12) in those days was $25 per pound. Most systems took two pounds of refrigerant, making the retail price a break-even, without labor and equipment costs factored in. The promotion was an immediate hit. It flooded the business with A/C work. We scheduled A/C services every half-hour, every day, for months.

The surrounding automotive businesses thought I was nuts. I was happy for them to believe that. What we knew though, was that the average repair was $800, not $49.95. Seldom will refriger-ant fix an air-conditioning problem. It's usually hardware: com-pressors, condensers, clutches, coils, high-side lines, low-side lines, O-rings, etc. Many people were willing to have us replace the items to keep themselves cool in the ninety-degree weather. Many weren't though, or couldn't. A number of people simply couldn't afford to pay the $800, $1,000, or sometimes $1,400 to repair their systems. I hated leaving money on the table. I was searching for an idea to capture a bigger piece of that revenue stream.

One rainy Saturday, my wife said, "You need to set up financing for those repairs." In addition to teaching, she worked at the busi-ness, running it whenever I wasn't there. She always had insightful, practical suggestions for things I'd struggle with. I thought that was a great idea. So, the following Monday morning, I started call-ing banks. One bank after another said that they didn't do that sort of financing. Discouraged, I made a few final phone calls. The last bank I called said "yes" immediately to the question. After hearing "no" almost a hundred times, I re-asked the question to be sure they heard the question correctly. "Yes," they repeated. I made an appointment to meet with the branch manager to better under-stand the entire process. They signed us up, gave us a store ID, and provided supplies that would allow me to offer financing on site. We could open up lines of credit (up to $10,000) in fifteen minutes, and offer customers ninety days without payments and interest. The customers would later receive a personalized credit card in the mail that could only be used at my dealership.

We immediately implemented the offer into the A/C process, offering every customer the opportunity to pay the balance in installments, and without interest if paid off within the first three months. The offer took off instantly. We learned that people would tend to consolidate and accelerate—what would have been mul-tiple purchases in the past—into a single "do it all now" purchase.

What was previously an average sale of $200 when customers used their own credit card, personal check, or cash, became an average sale of $800. That represented an incremental sale of $600, and an incremental profit of $420. The promotion was huge success. I was trying to figure out how to market it to the public. I knew it could become our primary method of differentiation, so I wanted to brand it. I trademarked: Repair Now & Pay Later!®

Based on the success we had in my little business, one day my wife said, "You need to figure out how to sell this." I hadn't given that a single thought, but when I did, I soon realized that if applied in a new car dealership, the return on investment could be huge. My wife had a communications degree and had worked in advertising prior to becoming an English teacher. She suggested that we try to get a story written about us to draw some attention to the process. She started working toward getting us some recognition in two major automotive publications: *Automotive News* and *Chilton's MotorAge*. In the meantime, I started thinking about how to package the concept to potential buyers. I ended up patterning the software industry. A build-it-once, sell-it-multiple-times model. With the trademark in place, I thought if I could simply license the use of the mark, I could then create the relationship between the dealership and the bank.

I met with the branch manager again to gauge his interest. As any business manager is, he was anxious to grow his businesses' revenues and profits, so he was fully cooperative. Coincidentally, around the same time, my wife had answered a call at our business from an owner of a repair shop a few towns over. He said he heard our radio commercial and would like to offer financing for his customers too. My wife made an appointment to go see the repair shop owner and make our first sale. Before going, she asked me, "How much is it?" I said I had no idea, and we proceeded to talk about how much we thought it should be. We settled on $3,000 for the first year, with a renewal fee of $1,000 for every year thereafter. She met with the repair shop owner later in the week, and walked out with a check for $3,000. That check was really our proof of concept with respect to the idea of selling the process. The approach itself was validated in our business's results.

With newfound confidence, I took a seven-line classified ad out in *Automotive News*, the flagship publication of the automobile business. That publication was on the desk of every dealer principal in every dealership in the country. "Imagine your sales business without financing for your customers," it began. "Now imagine your service business with it. Repair Now & Pay Later!®", and our toll-free number. The phone rang off the hook. We licensed our first new car dealership—a Chevrolet dealership—in Walden, New York. Shortly afterward, my wife was contacted by the editor of *Chilton's MotorAge*. They said they were interested in writing an article. With the commitment from Chilton, she contacted *Automotive News* and let them know that they might miss out on the story, as we already had an agreement with another publication. She was successful in getting their interest, and made arrangements for me to be interviewed by the person writing the story.

The next several years were a whirlwind. Within two years, we had dealerships using the process in forty-six states. Initially, we used the branch network of the bank, but that was complicated by the fact that each branch was chartered by its home state's laws. That necessitated having a different process in each state to fully comply with that state's rules and regulations. Once we were in about fifteen states, the bank suggested we port the business portfolio over to a sister-subsidiary company, which had a national charter. The importance and advantage that a national charter provided was the ability to "export" rates nationwide, and the fact that they were subject to only one set of laws. That allowed us to get back to one way of doing things. Something called the Internet was happening around then too. Being an early adopter of technology, I embraced the Internet and its facilitation of doing business at a distance. Until then, I was physically traveling to every location that licensed the use of the process. It wasn't unusual for me to be gone for twenty-five days at a time. I remember renting a car in Dallas for six weeks. When I returned the car, I had put nine thousand miles on it. In addition to reducing the travel expenses, I was able to change the fee structure, as well. We reduced the initial enrollment fee of $3,000 to $495, and rather that an annual renewal, we went to monthly subscriptions—$199 a month, on an open ended basis. Any use—submitting a credit application, accepting a card for payment, etc.—automatically extended the agreement. The reduction in the upfront cost reduced the perceived risk and accelerated the number of dealerships signing up.

With hundreds of dealerships using the process, cash flow was strong. Because our initial costs were covered by the initial enrollment fee, the additional monthly revenue stream was pure, so profitability was tremendous. That cash flow and profitability enabled me to work out of the giant hole I had created for myself, first with the mortgage on my relative's house, and then repaying my mother for the loan she made me to start the company.

Unfortunately, she didn't live to see it fully repaid. Over the years, she had been battling cancer. She lost her fourth bout, a skin cancer that metastasized to her liver. She called me the Sunday night before she died. I was in Texas, attending a NASCAR race at Texas Motor Speedway. It was one of the ways that I occupied myself during those twenty-five day trips. She asked me when I was coming home. I told her I was flying home on Wednesday and I would see her then. As she was hanging up, she said, "Have a nice trip," as if it would be weeks before she would see me again. I said, "Ma, I'll be home in a *couple of days*. I'll see you then."

"Okay," she said. "Bye." That would be the last time I talked to, or saw my mother alive.

The next day, Monday, I woke up with incredible stomach pain. I was scheduled to install the process at a dealership group in Austin, Texas. I never missed work, especially when I was on the road. I mean *never. Ever.* That day, I couldn't work. I hadn't missed a day like that before and haven't since. I just could not work that day. I called my office and had them re-schedule the dealership install for the following day.

That following morning, Tuesday, I got a phone call. It was my wife. My mother had slipped into a coma the night before and was unresponsive. She asked me to get home as soon as I could. It took me fourteen hours to get home. By the time I did, my mother was gone. I'm not sure if my mother could sense something coming when she called me that Sunday, but now I just wish I could have that conversation back. You never know when, or what, your last words to someone will be, but mine could have been kinder, more considerate . . . loving. I often hope the pain I felt that Monday was me bearing a little of her suffering and, in some small way, having eased her passing. She lived a hard life and deserved an easier end. If I'm being brutally honest though, there was a part of me that didn't want to be there for her. Payback for not being there for me when I was a child. Her neediness often offended me, because I could never allow myself to be needy. Her lack always eclipsing mine. That may be an astonishing admission of selfishness, resentment, and petulance, but the struggle was ever present, perfectly descriptive of the essence of conflict. We buried my mother on my son's fourth birthday, casting a pall on what should have been cause for a celebration. Then we got to work getting her affairs in order. As my wife and I were cleaning out her house, my wife found a note that my mother left for me. "Rick, I love you forever—Ma."

Profit attracts competition. That is an established economic principle. As Repair Now & Pay Later!® grew, we started to get the attention of some of the auto manufacturers and large banks. Soon, General Motors added a ninety-day pay option to their GM Goodwrench program, Ford Motor Company added the same to their Quality Care program, and BankOne launched something called CarCareOne. The factories' field representatives started asking their respective dealerships to cancel their contracts with us, and begin using their factory branded programs. It started to negatively impact my business and create unsustainable churn. Fortunately, I anticipated that the window was closing and planned an exit on my terms. My mother's death took a little of the wind out of my sails, and September 11th made traveling painful. I hadn't been to college at that point, something that I had wanted to do for a long time. My business would continue to throw off cash for the foreseeable future, so my time was my own. At thirty-six years old, I became a full-time college student.

My academic advisor said he never saw anyone chew through a program like I did. I had amassed about thirty credits prior to starting, by taking classes on and off over a couple years earlier, then took ninety credits in two years to finish a bachelor's degree in accountancy. I took as many classes as I could during each summer session and inter-session. I graduated Magna Cum Laude and had the highest GPA in my major. During the last undergraduate semester, I was taking seven classes and cramming for the GMAT exam, a requirement to get accepted to graduate school.

My undergraduate career wasn't without challenges. Sometimes, just as work or life had, the circumstances brought out my worst. The work was never the challenge—getting along with the people was. I remember taking my final exam in Intermediate

Accounting. The professor had given us a broad idea of what the exam would cover, but then was specific about what it wouldn't, allowing us to focus our energies on those broad areas. While sitting for the exam though, I found in the final pages exactly what he said wouldn't be covered. I was immediately incensed. He had specifically told us to ignore things that were now on the exam. I thought it was incredibly unfair. Beyond which, now it could negatively impact my grade and GPA. As soon as I saw it, I launched out of my chair and confronted him about it. I remember him saying, "Are you giving me shit?" I told him how unfair I thought it was, that I didn't appreciate it, and then sat down and finished the exam.

After class, he pulled me aside. He asked me what was going on. I told him how I felt about the unfairness of the material being on the exam. He told me not to worry about it, and that I had the highest grade in the class. He asked me why I was so wound up and suggested that I needed to calm down a bit, he thought I was putting too much pressure on myself. None of that made any difference to me. Like everything else in my life, I felt like it was a matter of survival, and he was messing with that.

The following semester, I took Advanced Accounting. During the first class, I remember the professor saying that her Cs were as good as anyone else's As. She also had a stipulation that certain study materials were only available to be viewed on campus, under supervision, and during specific times only. I was commuting to class, about forty-five minutes each way, and didn't appreciate the ninety-minute round trip necessary to comply with her restrictions. When I asked her about it, she couldn't have cared less about the impact on me. "It is what it is," she said. I felt like she was being incredibly inconsiderate, and made no effort to hide that fact. I offered to drop the class, which would have kept me from graduating on my tight timeline. She said that wasn't necessary, but did nothing to address the issue. I ended up with the lowest grade in my college career in that class, a C+. If I had been graded on how I handled the situation, I would have gotten an F.

I had taken all of the pre-requisites for the business school in the accountancy program, and after receiving my letter of acceptance, rolled seamlessly into full-time MBA studies. I finished graduate school with a 4.0 GPA in eighteen months, and graduated with a master's of business administration degree, with a concentration in finance. For me, the work was easy, I just got into a routine. I spent a half-day per class studying and doing homework. I treated it like a job, and I had always been good at work. I thought about a PhD program, and met with the head of a program I was interested in. I was conditionally accepted, but before I officially matriculated, I opted out. I didn't think I could commit five to seven more years meeting the requirements. Instead, I enrolled in a certificate of advanced graduate studies program in business intelligence.

I wasn't sure how I would reenter the workforce. I had no idea what I would end up doing. I went to college to give myself some options outside the automobile business, which was the only thing I knew. I got a call out of the blue one day—it was an invitation to interview for a process consulting gig for one of the domestic auto-mobile manufacturers. I responded with interest and scheduled an interview. I was fortunate enough to get hired and spent the next few years working with dealerships on process improvement initia-tives that would positively impact their customer's satisfaction.

I was assigned to twenty-two dealerships in the Rhode Island, Massachusetts, and Connecticut area. In some dealerships, there were other facilitators working with the same store, but assigned to their other brands. Occasionally, we would see each other and sometimes work together. There was one dealership I shared with another guy, and that dealership was pretty high maintenance.

The dealership's staff would call frequently, often during nights and weekends. I really didn't have a problem with that, as I prided myself on being available and responsive. But I started getting calls with questions about the other brand, which was the other guy's responsibility. They called me because he wouldn't call them back or respond to their emails. I'd do my best to answer their questions, but I didn't appreciate having to do the other guy's job.

Quarterly, we would go to Detroit to for a few days to meet with the automobile manufacturer and participate in workshops, spending time with colleagues and sharing best practices. During one of those visits, I voiced my displeasure about my having to handle the duties of the other facilitator to the project manager. This being my first experience in the corporate world, I was completely oblivious to the concept of corporate politics. When I didn't quite get the reaction I'd hoped for, I continued to harp on it, until she'd clearly had enough. I just felt like she didn't understand, so I wanted to make my point. It never quite got to the ugly stage, but it clearly got to the "not good" one. I just couldn't understand why she would condone that behavior. Later, I learned that the other guy had recently been diagnosed with cancer and was undergoing treatment. He was trying to keep it quiet, so it wasn't publicized. The project manager was worried for him, his health, and his family, and I was essentially attacking him, unknowingly. Unfortunately, the damage was done. I came across an insensitive jerk. What could have been a deployment of tact and diplomacy, wasn't. I was a bull in a china shop with respect to those delicate situations. I didn't understand nuance. I was about getting a job done and *only* getting a job done. If you were in my way, I would run you over.

I remember saying to her, "I'm just telling you like it is," or something close to that. When someone says, "I just call it like I see it," "I tell it like it is," or "I say what needs to be said," that's code for, "I believe my point of view is the only point of view;" "There can't be another point of view, especially one that is different than mine;" "The situation is the way it is, because that's the way I say it is;" "To me it is that way, and only that way;" "No amount of you saying it's different will change the way it is for me;" "The more energy you put into telling me it's different, the more energy I will expend to tell you you're wrong and defend the way I see it." Unfortunately, that single interaction alienated me from the group. I was always a black sheep anyway, given my history in the retail automobile business. Many of the facilitators had never worked in the industry, and the contract company viewed that background as a liability.

After spending a few years consulting in dealership's again, I found I missed the retail automobile business. If I'm being completely honest and transparent, though, what I really missed was making money. Business was good then, and dealership's managers were making three- to four-times more money than I was. I had been away from the retail business for a few years, but I felt that it might be time to get back in and max out my earnings. I still had cash flow coming from my credit card operation, which supplemented my income, but because I stopped enrolling dealerships years earlier, the cash flow diminished each month. I knew at some point it would stop altogether. I had an opportunity to go to work for a major regional dealer group. The group was comprised of about forty dealerships then, with almost every brand represented. I met with the owner of the group, and he said he didn't have a general manager making less than a quarter million dollars a year. I decided that the financial opportunity was worth it, so I hired on.

I was initially assigned to work with a general manager at one of the group's import dealerships close to home. I spent about four months learning the dealership group's ways; the tools, the processes, policies and procedures, etc. I was then assigned to an underperforming store. The store had lost about $330,000 the prior year and was undercapitalized as a result. The dealership had been run at a distance by a general manager who also ran dealerships a couple hours away. He would get to the dealership once or twice a week, but given his other responsibilities, he couldn't be there enough. The employees were running the place the best they could in his absence and had come to enjoy their autonomy. When I got there and started locking things down, they didn't like it at all. In their own way, they all started trying me on, searching for the boundaries. I had certain things that I wanted done on a daily basis: pulling handles at night to make sure all the cars were locked, parking trades before everyone went home so the parking spaces in front of the dealership were open for customers the following morning, etc.

One day, I asked a salesperson to do something . . . I can't even remember what now. But I do remember him telling me he wouldn't do it. At first, I just asked him to do it again, and again he said he wasn't going to do it. So now, I'm starting to spin up, and in true fuck-you guy style, I proceed to *tell* him what he *will* do, or that he'll be *getting the fuck out*. So, in addition to him telling me he isn't going to do it, he's in my face, and I can tell he's bracing for a confrontation. I'm not intimidated at all, but he's crowding me and being as physically threatening as he can be, and this is going on in the middle of the showroom. There was an instant, which I can only describe in football terms, when the frontline members of a team's defense are taking physical cues from the members of the opposing team's offense, and the movement of those offensive players dictates the defensive player's reaction. I reacted. It was automatic and thoughtless. I raised my hands and thrust my palms outward into his chest, shoving him away from me. It took a moment to sink in, and I could see the shock on his face. I had been in countless fights in my life, but I had never put my hands on someone during that type of disagreement.

Over the remaining course of the day, we worked it out. We

sat down and talked about it; we each apologized, and he said he wasn't sure that the business was the right fit for him. I told him that I completely understood; he was welcome to stay; that I saw abilities in him that he didn't see in himself, but if he stayed, he would have to do what I told him. That was part of it. It was nonnegotiable. I understood his doubt about the business being the right fit for him. I had my own doubts about it fitting myself. I didn't feel like I fit the company's culture, and the business brought out my worst. In the future, if someone asked me to tell them about a time that tended to bring out my worst, that turned me into that guy that I didn't want to be but was anyway— the question I often ask daily of others now—this time and the next several years would provide me with scores of examples.

My first act as general manager was to ask the holding company for a $250,000 loan so we could continue to operate. The dealership had only sold nine used cars the month before I got there. Given my background, that was the easiest thing to fix first. Within sixty days the dealership was selling close to forty used cars and profitable on a monthly basis. I was working seven days a week though, and I was tracking to make $100,000. My bonuses were jokes, because I wasn't paid on the lift from the deficit to zero, only on zero to above. I had been getting calls for other opportunities, and I wasn't getting along with the executive vice-president. In fairness to me though, I really feel like he wasn't getting along with me. Each time he'd see me, he'd bring up my MBA: "Why do you need an MBA, I don't have an MBA, look at me." As Gallup says, and I now preach: people don't quit companies, they quit managers. If an employee's relationship with their direct boss is broken, that employee will leave that company. I did just that.

I had an opportunity to work closer to home, and in a state that mandated all automobile dealerships close on Sundays. It would reduce my workweek from seven days to six, at the very least. The owner had a reputation for being a hothead—a polite way of saying a fucking maniac—but he was a self-made guy, had started at the bottom and worked his way up, and I respected that about him. The second Saturday I was there, we sold eighteen cars. It wasn't a dealership record, but it was close. I knew I was in trouble when, after learning how many total vehicles were sold, he asked, "How many *new* cars did we sell?" My pay plan paid me on gross profit; I couldn't have cared less about how many new cars, used cars, passenger cars, trucks, SUVs, what brands they were, which models of those brands . . . none of it mattered to me. What did matter to me was how much money we made selling them. For him though, it did matter. He prided himself on being number one in a brand for the entire state.

In hindsight, I'd say I jumped out of the frying pan into the fire when I took that job. We had completely different business philosophies, which we were never able to reconcile. He was tough on people—tougher than I was, which was saying something. One Saturday morning, he rolled in like a hurricane, vortices swirling around in his wake. He saw one vehicle slightly out of line along the side of the building. He walked in through the side door and flipped the nearest desk over, yelling at the top of his lungs that we were fucking lazy, stupid, and didn't pay attention to detail. He would get so worked up at times that he would literally foam at the mouth while telling us we were fucking idiots, and that he might replace us with his wife or kids. I found myself trying to be a buffer between him and the employees, which is weirdly comical because it was me that people usually needed to be buffered from.

The fact that I wouldn't pile on when he was lighting someone up for a minor infraction, he viewed as weakness. He felt I was protecting people. I guess I was; I just didn't feel the need to bully the vulnerable. If I was looking to pick a fight, it would be with the baddest motherfucker in the room. That was him, and I did. Given that it was his place and not mine, if one of us had to go, it wouldn't be him. And it wasn't . . . about eight months later, I was out. But I think I left holding the record for lasting longer than any other outsider, as they called me, ever had. The one positive thing it did for me, though, was give an opportunity to be on the other side of me for once. He was the only other person who shook a room the way I did when I flipped the fuck out. That was first time I can remember thinking: *Maybe my reactions aren't so good.*

The *first* Saturday I was there, we had a major snowstorm. Snow complicates life tremendously in the car business. It's not uncommon to have five hundred cars on the ground that need to be brushed off, moved, and re-moved after plowing the empty spaces. As we were all outside doing those things, one of the service advisors called my cell in a panic. The ceiling had collapsed in the Service Department write-up area, and water was pouring in from the roof. The computers were at risk of being damaged permanently by the water, and many of the paper documents were already destroyed. The service manager and I decided to get on the roof and shovel the snow away from that part of the building looking for any ice dams that may have formed. My wife called my cell for something, and I was trying to explain to her the chaos that was going on, that I was on the roof shoveling snow and couldn't talk. I called the owner, because I thought he should know what was going on. He showed up a couple hours later, asking me if I had already instructed everyone in the Service Department to work Sunday so that we could be ready for business Monday morning. I hadn't, so he did. "Listen," he said. "Everyone is working tomorrow. We need to get this place cleaned up for Monday. It's all hands on deck. That's how you do it." Then he left. The rest of us didn't leave until after midnight.

Late nights were routine, the dealership didn't close until 9:00 p.m., and we often still had customers in the building then. We were lucky to get out by 9:30 or 10:00, but it was often much later. The owner liked his general managers in the dealerships by 7:00 a.m., and he would call each morning to check. Getting home at 10:00 or 11:00 at night, then being back to work at 7:00 a.m., including an hour or so of commute each way, made that job a super-grind. The owner paid his people well, but used the income as a weapon. If you accepted a paycheck from him, he felt like he owned you, 24/7. I almost never took my day off, but when I did it was painful. I remember him calling me on my day off one day, flipping out about there being no intensity in the dealership when I wasn't there . . . code for *get your ass back to work if you want to keep your job.* The time started to be an issue at home. I was never home. My wife was working and trying to raise our son, and I know she sometimes felt like a single parent. She hated the business, mostly because of my behavior when she first met me. Working until close, and then hitting the bars, closing them, sleeping for a minute, and then getting back to work. I had left a job working four day weeks to get back into the retail business. She hadn't agreed with the decision, but didn't stand in the way of it.

After countless fourteen-hour days and ninety-hour work weeks, if my wife mentioned the time I wasn't home, I'd immediately spin up and flip out. "WHAT THE FUCK DO YOU THINK I'M DOING ALL WEEK, HAVING A FUCKING PARTY? I'VE GOT TO PAY FOR ALL THIS SHIT. WHO THE FUCK DO YOU THINK IS GOING TO PAY FOR IT, YOU?" The reactions were always the same: ferocious intensity, vehemence, profanity, condemnation, and verbal abuse. I'm sure my wife had no idea why I would become such a confrontational lunatic. I didn't understand it then either. I was so resentful that anyone dare question me about the time spent providing for my family, the mere mention of it was tantamount to fanning hot embers into a flame. She'd remind me that she worked too, and that would be like pouring water on a grease fire. "GREAT, YOU WANT ME HOME MORE? I'LL QUIT MY FUCKING JOB, AND WE'LL BE HOMELESS. WE'LL SHARE A FUCKING CAR, AND PUT OUR KID IN A PUBLIC FUCKING SCHOOL. WILL THAT MAKE YOU HAPPY? YOU WANT ME TO BE A FUCK-ING HOUSE HUSBAND, SITTING ON MY ASS, WATCHING TV, AND EATING FUCKING ICE-CREAM!" She often said that she didn't like the way I talked to her. Of course, I had selective memory and never remembered the outbursts, of which, there were many. Just writing this, I can't imagine how she continued to see the best in me. I'll never forget how she continued to love me, even when I was at my worst. I once asked her why she married me, and she said she saw potential in me. I wish I could have lived up to that potential sooner. I'm so sorry for all those years that I couldn't have been more.

Now, I completely understand what was going on. I've become an expert in working with reactions of this sort, no matter how extreme. My value of providing was offended. It is no more and no less than that. The intensity of my reaction would escalate, depending on whether I had been drinking, or whether the value offended tied back to me not being enough in some way. Had I understood at the time that my wife was simply behaving with respect to her values (family, harmony, or protectiveness perhaps) then I wouldn't have interpreted her behavior as a personal attack. I would have understood that perhaps I offended a value of hers, and maybe she was reacting herself. That reaction, in turn, created the behavior in me she didn't want, and resulted in the two of us reacting to each other in a continuous, endless loop.

The most liberating thing to know about conflict, though, is it can't exist if you don't participate in it. Like working through a Super Wicked Problem, understanding how you are participating, and stopping that participation, is the key. Interrupting a reaction is a function of the thinking brain, which is often shut down during an emotional hijacking. Like a train approaching a railroad switch, to master conflict one must train (no pun intended) oneself to intentionally choose one track versus the other. One leads to the reaction, and the other to a smarter, more productive outcome. We'll explore this in depth in the Refrain chapter.

STEP THREE–
EMOTIONAL REACTIONS

"There are some people who always seem angry
and continuously look for conflict.
Walk away; the battle they are fighting isn't with you,
it is with themselves."
—Anonymous

" I can't work with this guy anymore." Chris was referring to Brian. "I'd rather work alone. I can't get him to do anything I ask him to do. If he doesn't agree with what I decide, he doesn't want anything to do with the deal. He's fucking useless . . . pardon my language."

"When is the situation worst?" I asked.

"When we're in the middle of a deal. He'll always want to chime in . . . to offer his two cents."

"Like how, for instance?" I inquired.

"I don't know, he'll mumble something about, 'don't forget the rate, or this bank or that bank, or the rebates changed, or this car or that car;' and I'm like, I know that . . . shut the fuck up! Don't you have something else you could be doing? And then I'll want to send him in to close the deal, and he won't want any part of it. I'm telling you, the guy is fucking useless."

"What do you think is going on with him, when he's suggesting something?" I asked, checking Chris's interpretation of Brian's behavior.

"He must think I don't know what the fuck I'm doing. I don't need the help that way, you know. Just do what the fuck I tell you. It's simple."

Chris was obviously spun up. He was painfully unaware that he was reacting in Conflict by perceiving Brian's behavior as intentionally offensive. The situation wasn't working for them, and it wasn't working for the dealership either. The bottom line was that if we couldn't get this figured out, one or both of them had to go. For me, the situation was routine. I had lived it a thousand times in my life. It was crystal clear to me now, but I had forty-six years of doing the same thing before I figured it out. Working with individuals struggling with conflict is pretty straightforward. It adds another level of complexity though, when there are two people actively contributing to it. The steps are the same, but it requires working with one of the parties individually then the other, and then getting them together to work through it.

So, I began with Chris. "Chris, I'd like you to pretend you're describing yourself to a stranger; and you'd like that stranger to know everything about you that you'd want them to know in six, or eight, or ten words. What are those words?"

He struggled with the words, so we worked with the spirit of the words: personal responsibility (taking ownership of a situation), tenacity (not giving up), control (I know what I'm doing), and situational awareness (noticing things).

"Okay, great," I said. "Thank you. Chris, if Brian were here with us, and I asked the same question of him that I asked of you—to describe himself to a stranger—what do you suppose those words would be?"

"I don't know," he said, searching. "Maybe family, he doesn't seem to want to work the hours. Maybe independence, he doesn't do anything I tell him. Maybe stubbornness . . . "

The conversation wasn't going the way I'd hoped, so I had to get us back on track. "Chris, let's start fresh here. I want to remind you of some of the dynamics at play. First, please keep in mind that all human behavior is a function of personal values. Whatever Brian is doing, even though it may make no sense to you from a distance, please know that Brian is simply acting on behalf of his personal values. If you don't understand someone's behavior, you don't understand their personal values, and vice-versa; if you don't understand their personal values, their behavior may make no sense to you. Would you say that's true for you in Brian's case?"

"Yes," he admitted.

"Identifying personal values is important for a few reasons. First, because conflict exists when someone feels like one of their personal values has been offended; or, second, if one feels like another is imposing their personal values on them. But third, because when you declare your personal values, you are also identifying your triggers. And to compound this even further, sometimes we create the behavior we don't want in others by our reactiveness. Chris, you've said repeatedly that Brian won't do what you tell him."

"Well, shouldn't he?" he interrupted. "I am his boss."

"Sure," I said, not wanting to inflame the situation. "I would say that it is a fair expectation that an employee would follow the directions of their boss. But, I feel like there might be a few things going on here. Would it be okay if I share some things that I believe are complicating the situation between you two?" I asked permission to get his buy-in, otherwise I risked putting him on the defensive, and we'd make no progress. He'd simply dig in and defend his position and actions. The more I'd push to get him to see it my way, the more he'd push back to get me to see it his way. That would have added up to a lot of wasted time, and have become completely counter-productive.

"Sure," he said.

"Chris, earlier, you said one really important word."

"I did?"

"Any idea what it was?" I asked him.

"No, not really."

After a thinking a moment, I said, "You said *shouldn't*. Shouldn't Brian do what you tell him."

"Okay," he said, in a way that clearly indicated that he had no idea what I was talking about.

"What do you suppose that word indicates?" I challenged.

"I have no idea," he said, followed by a little nervous laughter.

"That word can indicate judgment. Meaning that when we hear ourselves using that word, it can alert us to the fact that we may be judging others based on our own personal value system. Would it surprise you to learn that, chances are, Brian will behave with respect to *his* personal values and not *yours*?"

"No, of course not," he said with complete understanding.

"Okay then, can you see how crazy it might be to expect and believe that Brian's behavior will fit *your* personal values and not *his*?"

"Yeah, I guess that makes sense," he said, while continuing to connect the dots in his head.

"So, if you don't understand Brian's behavior, you definitely don't understand his personal values. And whenever you hear yourself saying *should*, you are really saying another's behavior— in this case Brian's—is not in keeping with your personal values. When that's true, a personal value of yours is offended, and it's natural for you to spin up emotionally. Once spun up, you'll react either as a Victim or in Conflict. Would you say that you tend to withdraw, stop communicating, feeling helpless and powerless; or do you lash out, becoming angry and aggressive, argumentative and combative?"

"I definitely don't withdraw," he answered.

"Okay great," I said. "It's good that you can recognize that behavior in yourself. When you're reactive, you won't be your best self, you won't produce the best outcome, and you will do more to create the behavior that you don't want in others, rather than inspiring their cooperation. There's a big difference between force and power," I continued. "Force, is simply compliance at the end of a barrel. Do what I tell you, when I tell you, how I tell you, or get out; I'm in charge, I'm the boss. And it will only get you grudging compliance at best—that is, someone's absolute least, their bare minimum. Power, on the other hand, is inspiring their performance, setting the expectation and working with them, hand-in-hand, to get them there. Helping them achieve goals that they never believed that they could achieve on their own, lifting them up, building them.

Too often, managers approach their employees like a consultant approaches a business. The consultant arrives, conducts some kind of analysis, identifies a performance gap, prescribes a solution, and then tries to get everyone to execute on that idea. It becomes about the consultant themselves, their background, their experience, what they think, their fix, their agenda. It's all about *how* to do something. The real truth, though, is that no amount of knowing how to do something matters until someone *wants* to do it. The consultant can't want it for them, that's why consulting often fails to be durable over time. Once the consultant is gone, so is the impetus behind executing their solution. It's no different with employees; if they don't want to do something, it isn't going to get done.

Coaching focuses on the *want* to. Identifying the inherent drive that exists within all of us, and partnering with that person to help them achieve those things that are important to them in their lives. It attaches them to that purpose, and then work becomes the method that allows them to achieve those things. When that's true, they pour themselves in and give everything they've got, every day. Once they understand that their performance at work is necessarily tied to whether or not they will achieve their goals in their lives, you'll get their full cooperation. They will *pull* you along with them, rather than you feeling like you need to be *pushing* them. Would you say it's true that you feel like you need to *push* Brian?"

"Absolutely," he said, without hesitation.

"Okay, so my advice would be to try to go deeper with him."

"Shouldn't he do it for the money?" he asked rhetorically.

Without pointing out the "shouldn't" word again, I suggested, "Everyone works for money. The money they earn provides for the life they live. But it can't be *just* for the money. There has to be some reward in the work itself. If the work itself is not rewarding and fulfilling, the money will never be enough. People are like batteries. If they are a good fit, and possess the strengths that the role they fill demands, and they like the people they work with, and the people they work for, and they believe their personal values are alive in the organization they work in, and they are good at the work, then that charges their battery. It will sustain them over time; it will allow them to continue to do the job for the long term. If those things aren't true, it will drain their battery, leading to burn out. Their performance will suffer, and they will either self-select out, or you will end up asking them to leave. Again, though, the most powerful approach is trying to understand what they want to accomplish in their lives, and then partnering with them to help them accomplish those things. What do you suppose that might be for Brian?" I asked.

"I have no idea," Chris said, in a way that said the mere thought of the conversation with Brian exasperated him. "He probably wants my job," he said. Then after the slightest pause, "You're the Coach, what do you think?" smiling, with a tinge of condescension.

"I'll share what I think, and provide an example of what I'm talking about, but I'm not letting you off the hook that easy. The stuff we're talking about today is important for your future, Brian's future, and the dealership's future. I'm going to ask you again, so I'd like you to give it some serious thought.

My parents divorced when I was one," I began. "I met my father when I was twenty-seven. We never really had a relationship, still don't. Because I never had a relationship with my father, my relationship with my son is one of the most important things in life to me. Since he was born, it has been my mission to provide him a better start than I got. Chris, what do you suppose I'll allow to get in my way of providing my son a better start in life than I had?" I asked.

"What do you mean, get in the way?" he replied.

"Do you think if I hit traffic this morning, I would give up on providing him a better start?"

He shook his head side-to-side.

"If it rained today, do you think I'd give up? If it's too warm, or too cold, or snowing, or my flight is delayed, do you think any of those things stop me from providing him a better start?"

He was motionless.

"Death," I said. "My death is the only thing that will physically stop me from providing him a better start in life. And work is the way that I provide that better start for him. I'm keenly interested in anything that makes me more effective, that will elevate my performance, produce a better outcome. Why? Because the more successful I am at work, the brighter my son's future becomes. Can you see how I am attached to that purpose? If you were my boss, and I was underperforming, can you see the power in knowing my purpose? Your conversation with me, then, wouldn't only be about the money I could lose due to doing a substandard job. You could gently remind me that I was putting my son's future in jeopardy. Knowing how committed I am to that purpose, and reconnecting me to it, is eminently more powerful than highlighting the loss of some compensation alone. We all have those things in our lives. The challenge is to take the time, make the investment, to understand what that is for each and every person working for you. So, back to the original question," I stated. "What are those things for Brian?"

"I'm not sure," he said. "I never thought about it. I would need to have a conversation with him to figure those things out."

"Okay, great. Sounds like a good first step," I commended. "Before that though, we still have a little work to do on the relationship.

Chris, we began our conversation earlier with you declaring your values. And then you explained a situation that tended to bring out your worst. The situation you described had to do with you, when working a deal. During which, Brian would offer you a suggestion, and you would . . . " I was waiting for him to fill in the blank.

"I guess I would lash out, right?" he said, seeking my reinforcement.

"Yes, I think we would both agree that you tend to lash out, in that circumstance. What do you believe leads to your lashing out?" I asked him.

"My value was offended," he said tentatively.

"Great. Yes, one of your personal values was offended." I added, "Which one?"

"Wow . . . which one," he repeated. "I never thought about that."

"Well, let's think about it now, together," I instructed. "You said that after he's made his suggestion, you'll reply, 'I know that.' And, 'Don't you have something else you could be doing?' Of the personal values—personal responsibility, taking ownership of a situation; tenacity, not giving up; control, I know what I'm doing; situational awareness, noticing things—which one do you believe was offended?"

"I guess it could be control—I know what I'm doing, or personal responsibility—taking ownership of a situation, or maybe both."

"Okay, great. What is it about Brian's behavior that offends those values?"

"He tells me things that I already know; he just slows down the deal. When a salesperson is at the desk, I don't want them confused. Only one person can work a deal at a time. I don't want him butting in, so I tell him to shut up."

"And do you feel like his behavior is intentional?" I probed.

"Yes, it must be," he said. "He does it every time."

"Do you feel like the situation becomes emotionally loaded then?" I asked him.

"Of course, I'm pissed," he said.

"Okay, I understand," I said. "Let's break off for now, I want to spend some time with Brian, and then we'll all get back together later."

"Alright, good enough," he said, as he was leaving.

"Hey Brian, what's going on man?"

"How are you?" he replied.

"Michael asked me to spend some time with you and Chris today," I said. "How's the vibe between you two?"

"Not so good. We don't work well together."

"What's going on?" I asked, trying to keep it light and casual.

"We just clash, you know?" he said. "We have different styles. He's a little bit of a control freak. He won't let me near the desk; forget about working a deal. I'm a sales manager, you know. That's part of my job. He wants to desk every deal. I try to give him my input, you know, I want to help. But he's not interested; he doesn't want to hear it. He just tells me to shut the fuck up. And then he'll ask me if there's something else I should be doing. Then, if the salesperson can't close the deal, he'll want me to go in and close it. By that time, the deal is already down the wrong road. I'm not going to be responsible for it when I can't contribute to the direction it's heading, you know. It's not fair. Then, he'll blame *me* if I don't close the deal. And I want to say, 'You structured this thing. If it doesn't work, it's not my fault.' But he's the boss, you know. I can't say that to him, he'll just flip out."

"Brian, I'd like to dig into this a little more deeply with you if that's okay," I requested.

"Sure," he said. "Any help you can give me, I'd greatly appreciate."

"Okay, so let's start at the beginning. To tee this up, I'm going to ask you a couple of questions that may seem a little odd, but I ask them the way I do on purpose, and as we go forward, I'll connect the dots for you. Ready?" I checked.

"Ready," he said.

"Brian, I'd like you to pretend you are describing yourself to a stranger; and you'd like that stranger to know everything about you, that you'd want them to know, in six, or eight, or ten words. What are those words?"

Like Chris, Brian struggled with the words, so we dealt with the spirit of the words: helpfulness (I want to help and contribute), empowerment (have some control over circumstances), accountability (being responsible for an outcome), and feeling valued (acknowledgment of my worth).

"That's great, Brian. Thank you. Now I'd like you to tell me about a situation that tends to bring out your worst, that turns you into that person that you don't want to be, but are anyway."

"At work or at home?" he asked me.

"It can be either," I answered. "It won't make a difference in our conversation. You decide."

"Well, since we're taking about work, let's keep it about work."

"Good enough," I said. "So what's the situation?"

"I'll give you two guesses," he said. "We just talked about it.

When Chris and I are at the desk, and he insists on working every deal, excluding me, holding me accountable for things that I have no say in, telling me to shut the fuck up, being demeaning and dismissive. That's the worst. I just want to pack my shit and go home, you know. I feel worthless."

"Okay, thank you for sharing that, Brian. A little bit ago, I said that I would ask you a couple of questions, and then connect the dots as we went forward. So, here are how the dots connect." I explained personal values, reactions, and triggers to Brian as I did to Chris. "Any of this sound familiar, Brian?"

"Sounds like you described exactly what's going on with me and Chris," he said.

"How do you think it fits?" I asked.

"Well, for one, Chris reacts in Conflict. He lashes out. And I react as more of a Victim, I'd say. I do feel powerless. And that thing about the behavior in others, he definitely does that with me."

"What are the personal values that are coming into play here, Brian?"

"For me or for Chris?"

"For you," I responded.

"Well, helpfulness for one. He doesn't want my help," he said, discouraged.

"Would it surprise you to learn that when I met with Chris, he said that he thought when you were trying to make suggestions, you were doing so because you didn't think he knows what he is doing?"

Stunned, Brian exclaimed, "Are you kidding me? That's what he thinks? Nothing is further from the truth. I know he knows what he's doing. I just want to contribute. I get paid to do a job; I want to do it."

"What other personal values do you think are coming in to play?" I asked.

"The accountability one, for sure," he said. "I have no problem being accountable, unless I have no say in what's going on. If I can't take part in setting things up, I'm not going to be responsible for what happens. At that point, I don't want any part of it."

"Do you think Chris understands that about you?"

"Obviously, not," he stated. "He doesn't understand that I don't want to go into a deal that I had no part in structuring. Because, when it crashes, he blames me . . . and it was him that set it up that way in the first place. He should just go in himself at that point."

"Brian, when people use the word *should* it indicates that they are judging a situation in a way that is in keeping with their own personal values. Do you think you and Chris share the same personal values?"

"Boy, it sure doesn't seem like it," he said, genuinely.

"So, if that's true then, you and Chris have different personal values, leading to you each behaving differently in keeping with those personal values, is it any wonder that Chris's behavior might be different than yours in a given situation?"

"No, I guess not."

"Can you see now how your behavior might offend a personal value of his, and his behavior might offend a personal value of yours?"

"Yes, I believe that's true," he said, nodding in agreement.

"And when that happens, you each emotionally load the situation, which leads to reactions and creating the behavior in each other that you both don't want. It can fast become an endless loop, resulting in lose/lose outcomes for the two of you. Not to mention for your employees and the dealership in general."

"I would say that's true," he conceded.

"Okay, let's work on changing that then. I'm going to ask Chris to join us, and we'll try to get this thing figured out."

"So, here's the deal, guys," I began. "I was asked by Michael to work with you both today. I worked with you, Chris, this morning and with you, Brian, this afternoon. Now, we're going to spend some time together to try to figure this thing out. Based on our individual conversations, I would say it's no secret that your working relationship could be better. Michael believes that it is negatively impacting the Sales Department and the dealership in general. He also believes it's become tough for the employees, specifically salespeople, when you guys don't get along. I have a ton of experience dealing with this dynamic, and I believe we can get this handled, but know this: If it doesn't improve, one or both of you will be gone. So, that being said, are you both willing to fully participate and work through the challenges that you're both creating for each other?"

"Creating for each other?" Chris asked, a little perturbed.

"Yes, creating for each other," I repeated. "We'll get to that in a moment. I want you both to commit to bargaining in good faith. Bargaining in good faith means that you will remain solution oriented and assume a positive intent. That means you are steadfast in the belief that each party wants what's best for the other party, along with producing the best mutual outcome."

"I'm willing," Brian spoke up.

"Yes, I'm willing," Chris followed.

"Okay then," I acknowledged. "When I met you each individually, you each referred to a situation that brought out your worst. Coincidentally, the situation that you each referred to was the same one. It had to do with how the deals at the desk were being worked, and the dynamic between you both while working those deals."

I turned to look at Chris. "Chris, you referred to the fact that when you were working a deal, Brian would often offer you some suggestions that you believed simply slowed down the deal, confused the salespeople, and it was often stuff that you already knew."

I addressed Brian next. "Brian, you explained that Chris wouldn't find your suggestions helpful or useful and would be dismissive of them, and you. But, shortly afterwards, Chris would want you to go in and close the deal, structured in a way that you had no part of. If you weren't able to close the deal, Chris would blame that outcome on you.

What we're really doing here today, guys, is trying to heighten your self-awareness. Elevate it in a way that you understand how your own behavior is actually part of the problem. I told you each separately that sometimes we create the behavior in others that we don't want. I believe you are each doing that to the other. We're also trying to raise your awareness of others by helping you see how another's behavior is simply a function of their personal values, which should eliminate the perceived offensiveness of their actions.

Chris, you said that you believe Brian makes suggestions while you're working a deal because he doesn't think you know what you're doing. Is that true?"

"Yes, Chris answered. "I think that's true."

"Okay, great. Brian, would you please explain to Chris what's at play for you when making suggestions to him while he's working a deal?"

"I just want to contribute," he began. "It has nothing to do with me thinking that you don't know what you're doing; I know you know what you're doing. But I'm a sales manager too, and when we're both at the desk, you want to work every deal. I feel like I can't participate. And then you structure the deal in a way that I might not and want to send me in to the customer, and I might not agree with the way it's being structured. At that point, I don't want anything to do with it. I have no problem being accountable, or responsible, for a deal that I have some say in, but I don't want to be responsible for something that I have no part in. And then you tell me to shut the fuck up, and go do something else . . . I feel like a piece of shit at that point; I just want to go home. And if you do ask me to get involved, the deal is already put together, and if it doesn't go well with the customer, you blame me. It sucks."

There was a long period of silence. I had to prompt Chris to respond.

"I can see that," he said, deflated. "I'm probably guilty of that."

"I appreciate that, Chris," I said. "Owning it is a big part of it. *Changing* it is the other part. Brian, you said that if you can't take part in structuring the deal, you don't want any part of it at that point. Is that true?"

"Yes," he said, "that's how I feel."

"Chris, can you share how you feel about Brian's aversion to taking part in a deal that he hasn't structured?"

"Brian is a talented sales manager. He's really good in front of a customer. They love him. The last thing we want to do is have two guys doing one job, and I feel like that's what it would be if we were both working deals. There's plenty for both of us to do, and some of what needs to get done isn't getting done. I'd rather have Brian concentrating on doing one-on-ones with salespeople, following up on unsold customers, training salespeople on the sales process and product knowledge, and being able to plug him in to any deal, anytime, as necessary. That would be the smartest and best use of his abilities and talents. And I run the department. I need him to support the decisions that I make. He can't just sulk, or disappear, if he disagrees with something I'm doing. We need to be able to have a conversation about it. But he tends to shut down, which makes talking about it difficult."

Again, silence. "Brian?" I prompted. There wasn't a response right away.

"Yeah," he said, finally. "I would say I do that."

"Okay," I announced. "Great, good job, guys. This stuff isn't easy. We're talking about you and your personal values, your reactions, and behavior; it's natural for it to be emotional. But you both owned your part, which is great. As I said before, that's a big part of it. But the most important part is talking about what we're going to do about it.

Chris, what are some ideas that come to mind, which might heal up the relationship and lead to a more productive environment going forward?"

"I think we need to get clear about who's going to do what," he suggested. "A clearer job description, for both of us. I'm off one day a week, I'm at the auction one day a week, and I don't work Sundays, so there's plenty of opportunity for Brian to desk deals. We probably need to compare our styles a little more closely. The last thing we want is for salespeople to have to learn two ways of doing things depending on who's on the desk. If Brian is offering me something during a deal, I guess I don't have to be such an asshole about it. And before sending him into a deal, I could ask for his input about how it's structured, then not blame him for the outcome."

"And when will you begin that Chris?" I asked.

"When we go downstairs . . . I'll do my best to start fresh."

I turned to Brian and asked what he thought.

"I'm willing to start over," he said. "I guess I can try to be more involved in the deals that I don't desk, as long as I know something about them before I go in. I know there's more to do than desk deals, and there are things that aren't getting done. They need to get done too. But when someone tells me to shut the fuck up, I have no motivation to go do those things. So, if the dynamic is better between us, I'll be more motivated to get the other stuff done."

"Brian," I asked, "are you willing to begin immediately?"

"Yes, I'll start over immediately."

"Okay, I think we've made some progress here today. We'll revisit this when I'm back next. I'd like you both to keep a record of any situation where you find yourself spun-up. Use whatever works—some people use a journal, some a legal pad, some keep it on their phones—I don't care how, just as long as you do it. When I return, we'll take a look at those situations together. We'll deconstruct them like we did today. The same forces will be at work—

personal values, emotionally loaded situations, reactions as a Victim or in Conflict—and we need the specifics of the situations to understand what's at play. That's the purpose of documenting them. We didn't have time today, but we'll also discuss how to interrupt the reactions, and transform the negative emotional reactions into positive responses. That flips the entire interaction from negative to positive, from win/lose to win/win. I appreciate your participation today, and I know Michael does as well. I already can't wait to hear about and celebrate your progress."

REFRAIN:
THE THEORY OF REACTIVITY

*"Peace cannot be kept by force; it can only
be achieved by understanding."*
—Albert Einstein

It's incredible to me how often I hear the very words that I said myself, while participating in the training at iPEC, said back to me by people that I coach on conflict. Recently, I was working with someone who was trying to explain their reactiveness. "I can't control it," they said. "It just happens, it's already happened before I can think about it happening. It's like a reflex. I don't think I can change that."

"Of course, you can change it," I assured them with absolute conviction, in an effort to share my confidence with them. My confidence was justified. I know it can be changed. I had changed it in myself. For years before, I was stuck in a loop of loops, a chain of reactions; my behavior creating the behavior in others I didn't want. Their behavior creating that for them, in me. Thankfully, that's no longer true, as I've come to *understand* my way out.

Several years earlier, I had a conversation that sounded remarkably the same. The iPEC Coach Instructor was hosting a conversation about personal limitations, challenges, and things about ourselves we would like to be different. We went around the room, sharing those shortcomings, like pointing out the defects in a product or service. When it was my turn, the instructor asked me to share mine. I talked about being reactive, like a compressed coiled spring. That analogy was apt, due to a compressed coiled spring's characteristic of storing potential energy. That is energy stored impatiently, waiting to be released. I explained how my reactions were seemingly instantaneous, often happening before I could even perceive them occurring and how I couldn't fathom trying to manage that. She shared some techniques with me that she found effective at physically interrupting her reactions; taking a breath, taking a walk, counting to ten, counting Mississippis, etc. Her suggestions were moderately helpful. I found that, over time, I could interrupt my reactions using those techniques. But interrupting the reactions and no longer being reactive were different things entirely. I didn't want to simply interrupt them; I didn't want them to exist.

In my view, interrupting reactivity is the most difficult step in the entire five-step process. It's the one that I spend the most time with Coachees on, and the one that is the most difficult for people to understand and practice. There are two degrees of interruption. The first interrupts the reaction, but the source emotion remains. People who get to this level will be less reactive, to the point that others will notice and comment about the behavioral changes they've seen in that formerly reactive person. Those formerly reactive people will have taught themselves to physically restrain the reaction. It's a good first step, and for some people, enough, wholly determined by the number and frequency of interactions with others. The problem, though, is that one can wear through one's restraint. Restraint, like will power, is an exhaustible resource. If one is faced with repeated situations that require restraint on an ongoing basis, at some point, the restraint will fail, and the reaction will occur. So, a more peaceful existence requires additional work.

The next level eliminates the reaction entirely, by first eliminating the source emotion. People who get to this level will no longer be reactive. The comments about them will be of disbelief and awe. When the source emotion doesn't exist, there is no fuel to propel the reaction. Like a fire can't burn without oxygen, reactions can't occur without emotion. Sounds easy right? Not so much.

I'm going to wind us back to the beginning, to revisit the steps to get here, and then we'll go forward. During Step One, we identified our personal values by imagining we were describing ourselves to a stranger. By declaring our personal values, we also revealed our triggers. We learned that conflict exists when someone feels like one of their personal values was offended or if someone feels like another is imposing their personal values on them. During Step Two, we singled out certain hot situations that we discovered were prone to offending one of those personal values. In Step Three, we recognized our default reaction, either as a Victim or in Conflict, and examined the aftereffects of that behavior. Now, during Step Four, we will explore the ability to interrupt the emotions leading to the reaction and nullify the harsh consequences before they can arise. A little like traveling back in time, finding a person destined to commit some heinous act, and stopping their birth. As Sun Tzu advises, "The supreme art of war is to subdue the enemy without ever fighting."

Einstein said, "If you can't explain it simply, you don't understand it well enough." He used $E=mc^2$ to describe mass-energy equivalence; where E represents energy, m represents mass, and c^2 represents the speed of light (in a vacuum) squared. His theory of special relativity postulated that the mass of an object in motion would continuously increase as that object approached the speed of light. In real terms, earlier I referred to myself as feeling like a compressed coiled spring. Einstein would explain that, based on his theory, the mass of that compressed coiled spring would be greater than that of any uncompressed coiled spring, due to the motion of that coiled spring's compression and the energy stored in it as a result.

$E=mc^2$ was emblematic for Einstein in demonstrating the simplicity of the relationship between mass and energy. I am going to adapt his formula to demonstrate the simplicity of the relationship between emotional energy and the reactions that drive conflict. For me, it's a Theory of *Reactivity*, rather than one of relativity. *E*, in our case, will become **E²: Emotional Energy**, rather than Einstein's kinetic energy. **M** for us, will be **Magnitude**, rather than mass. And c^2 will become **C**, representing a **Constant**, which the speed of light was.

In words, the equation for a human emotional reaction differs a little from an atomic one, but is still no less characteristic of a chain of reactions. So, rather than "energy equals mass times the speed of light squared," our equation is **"emotional energy equals the magnitude of the reaction times the constant," E²=MC.** Working backwards, C represents the Constant. For Einstein, that was the speed of light. And the speed of light in a vacuum is referred to as a Universal Constant. For us, **the Universal Constant is our personal values set.** Like light speed in a vacuum, adapted from the Reaction chapter just to put a fine point on it—Light speed in a vacuum in the cosmic sense is no different than personal values in the human sense. It is ubiquitous, ever-vigilant, pervasive, and limitless. There is no waking up one day and contemplating choices based on the absence of it. It *is*. Likewise, personal values *are*. If one of your personal values is honesty, for example, it won't occur every other Tuesday at 10:00 a.m. Or every second Saturday. Or when it's sunny and warm. Or when vacationing in Alaska. If honesty is a personal value, you will *always* behave honestly, and you will expect the same of others—in our case though, it's *the specific* personal value that was offended. If multiple personal values are in play, which can be true, C^x would serve to indicate that. M, for us, symbolizes Magnitude and is a polynomial. **Magnitude is the product of the intensity (i) of the emotion, with respect to the perceived offense of one's personal values, multiplied by any history (h) that might exacerbate that perceived offense; like my abandonment issues, for example.** So, the Emotional Energy (E^2) available to fuel a physical reaction equals the magnitude of the reaction to the perceived offense (M)—which is itself the product of the intensity (i) of the reaction, multiplied by any history (h) that might predispose one to being hypersensitive to that offense—multiplied by the constant (C), which is the specific personal value. So mathematically, we'd write $E^2=((i)(h))(C)$, where $(i)(h) = M$.

Now, if you're not mathematically inclined, I'm sure your hair hurts right now, and you're wondering what the hell I'm talking about. I talk about it this way, and precisely this way, because it promotes our overall understanding of how conflict works. Permitting the identification and isolation of where our efforts to manage conflict will be the most effective and do the most good.

So, let's break it into its parts. If we wanted to materially impact conflict, given how I've described it mathematically, we might first look at E^2, Emotional Energy. Emotional Energy is the byproduct, a result, and a lagging indicator. It can't be managed directly because, by its very nature, on whatever scale we'd use to measure it, its quantity is necessarily determined by the amount of prior inputs. Hence, a more effective strategy in managing any effect would be by first focusing on that effect's cause. So, let's shift our focus to the other side of the equals sign and concentrate on the easier of the two; that's C, representing the Universal Constant. And let's pause for a moment before continuing.

Okay, now let's proceed slowly. I'd like you to make a list of all of the ways that you can think of to slow down, speed up, or change the constant speed of light. Ready? Go.

Wait a minute, there's nothing on your list. Okay, let's try a different example then. This time, make a list of all of the ways that you can think of to change the force of gravity. Ready? Go.

Hey! Another blank list, right? Values are just like that. You won't wake up one day and decide that integrity is no longer important to you. You won't change your behavior so that it's no longer in keeping with integrity. You are your values; your values are you and your behavior. So, if we can't impact the Universal Constant, and we can't impact the result, where should we concentrate our efforts?

Well, let's continue with Magnitude. Magnitude is made up of the intensity (i) of the emotion, with respect to the perceived offense of one's personal values, multiplied by any history (h) that might exacerbate that perceived offensiveness. Let's take the last one first; (h) represents history. Things that happened to us in the past make us who we are. I've spent most of this book sharing the things that happened to me. Just like we did for Constant, let's spend a few minutes listing all the things that we can do to change what's happened to us. I'll even give you a little more time. How does eternity sound? Even if I could give you an infinite amount of time—short of you inventing time travel, traveling back in time, undoing what was done, and returning to the present—no amount of time given would change anything that had already been done to you. *You can manage the future* based on those experiences, *but you can't manage the past.* So we're quickly running out of things to try to materially impact that will result in elevating our ability to manage conflict. There's only one left: (i) representing the intensity of the emotion, with respect to the perceived offense of one's personal values. And that's precisely why I crafted the explanation the way I did. It's the only thing that *can* be managed. *It's the only thing that ever could be managed.*

Let's get back to the math for a moment. What does eleven times zero equal? Go ahead, do it long hand, carry the one . . . right, zero! Okay, let's try a trickier one. What's 477,912 times zero equal? Done yet? Yes, zero! Okay, last one. What does infinity minus one, times zero equal? I intentionally used infinity minus one, so not to offend any real math wonks, who would certainly disagree with infinity times zero actually equaling zero. I don't think they would challenge the former statement, however. So if you answered zero, you were right! Again, you're wondering what the hell I'm talking about. I get it, enough math. The point I'm so painstakingly trying to make, maybe even painfully trying to make, is: **if the intensity (i) of the emotion, with respect to the perceived offense of one's personal values, *were zero*, then E^2=MC, *would necessarily reduce to zero*. As such: E^2=((i)(h)(C). E^2=((O)(h)) (C). E^2=(O)(C). E^2=O.**

In words: If I do not perceive another's behavior to be intentionally offensive, and no value of mine is offended, emotional energy will not be created. If there is no emotional energy created, there's nothing to load onto situations, so there can be no emotional reaction. Without an emotional reaction, I will remain solution oriented, seeking the smartest outcome, and remaining my best self.

Hopefully, I've convinced you that our only hope in managing conflict is eliminating the emotion that exists when one feels like one of their personal values has been offended. If that's true, then we should agree that putting all of our efforts into interrupting the reaction, by eliminating that emotion, is the most practical and effective approach.

Like in Einstein's theory of special relativity, the speed of an object is relative, given a person's position in respect to that object. Emotional reactions are also relative. A situation that offends the personal values of one person may not offend another. A situation that offends that other person, may offend someone else tenfold, given their history with that situation or hypersensitivity to that particular personal value. Regardless of the relative nature, though, interrupting the reaction by reducing the perceived offensiveness of another's behavior works. Its helpfulness, in turn, will be relative, with respect to the amount of emotion it is extinguishing.

STEP FOUR—INTERRUPTING EMOTIONAL REACTIONS

"And now, excuse me while I interrupt myself."
—Murray Walker

"Hey, what's going on, Peter? How's business?"

"Business is good," he said. Peter was one of the department managers at one of the dealerships I had been working with. "I need you to work with Joe today."

"Sure, no problem," I said. "What's going on with him?"

"I'm not really sure," he said. "I just feel like he isn't committed to me, the department, or the dealership. I'd like to try to get that figured out and get him onboard."

"What are some of Joe's behaviors that have you feeling this way?"

"Well, he's a time-clock watcher, for one," he began. "He's here every day at 7:59:59 a.m., waiting to punch in at 8:00 a.m., and he's at that clock at 4:59:59 p.m., waiting to punch out at 5:00. He always does a good job when he's here; he never misses work; but he just won't give me one extra second, EVER! Not ever," he repeated for emphasis. "It really pisses me off. I could really use the help; *we* could really use the help. I just can't count on him to be here extra if I need him. I just need him to step up more. Sorry to vent. This really bothers the shit out of me, though."

By his emotion, I could tell that this was a hot situation for him. I decided that I would work on his triggers after I spent some time with Joe.

"Is there anything else about Joe's behavior that leaves you believing that he isn't committed to you, the department, or the company?" I asked, seeking additional clarification.

"No," he said, matter-of-factly. "That's it."

"Okay, great," I said. "I'll spend some time with Joe, and circle back with you afterwards."

"Sounds like a plan," he said, smiling.

"Hey, Joe, how are you?"

"I'm good. It's been a little while. Business has been strong, we've been really busy, there just aren't enough hours in the day, you know."

"How's Peter been?" I asked, checking in on the temperature of the relationship between them.

"He's been good," Joe said. "A little stressed out, you know . . . we all are."

"What's causing the stress?"

"We're down a guy . . . remember Tom? He took a job as a manager down the street. We haven't been able to replace him. And you know this job takes forever to learn. I'm not sure how we're going to replace him," he said, somewhat resigned. "The rest of us have to pick up the slack. But, you know the deal, not everyone does."

"How have the hours been?"

"Fine," he replied.

"Any shot of overtime . . . to boost that paycheck?" I explored.

"Yeah, that would be great," he said. "I really can't though, you know . . . not with Emily. She's four now. After the divorce, my schedule got pretty tight. I'm a single parent, and I have full custody now. It makes it tough. I would love to do more. And I feel like I'm letting Peter down, but I have a kid I'm responsible for too. I do the best I can to try to balance everything. I get her to daycare as soon as they open, at 7:30 a.m., and it takes me between twenty and twenty-five minutes to get to work, depending on traffic. They close at 5:30 p.m., so I have to be out the door, right on time, to get there before they close . . . plus, whose kid wants to be last one to get picked up, you know? It's constant, man . . . I'm always running. I'm lucky to get here every day on time, but I do it . . . I make sure I'm never late."

"Sounds like you're making it work," I said. "Does Peter know about your situation with Emily?"

"You know, I'm not sure," he answered. "He has a lot on his plate right now; he's been really overwhelmed. He's been short with me lately, too, so I just try to stay out of his way. I don't need a target on my back, you know."

"Would it be okay with you if I shared some of this with Peter later?" I asked Joe.

"It's fine," he said. "I'm not trying to make any excuses, it's just what it is right now."

"Okay, thanks man, I appreciate it," I said. "Sounds like you're doing an amazing job with Emily . . . keep it up," I encouraged.

"So, I had a chance to meet with Joe," I said.

"Yeah, how'd that go?" Peter asked.

"I thought it went great," I replied. "Can we talk about it?"

"Give me fifteen minutes," Peter said. "I still have a guy at lunch."

"Okay, I'll return some phone calls and meet you back here in fifteen," I agreed.

When we finally sat down, Peter began by asking me, "So, did Joe explain why he can't be committed?"

"We talked about a lot of things," I said, being intentionally non-specific. "What are some of your struggles with the other employees?"

"Some of the guys are late," he said. "It's not really a big deal. It's not all the time, so I don't blow it up. Shit happens, you know. Sometimes, I'm late," he added. "But regardless of what time I get here, I'm here until the work is done. So are most of my guys. That's why it bothers me so much that Joe won't hang in when I need him."

"Peter, would it be okay if I shared with you an approach I use that might help level up your ability to understand your guys and their behavior?"

"Sure," he said, clearly not knowing what to expect.

"I'm going to begin by asking you two questions. These questions may sound a little strange; I promise I'll connect the dots for you as we go forward, but I ask them the way I do on purpose."

"Okay, shoot," he said.

"Peter, I'd like you to pretend you are describing yourself to a stranger, and you'd like that stranger to know everything about you, that you'd want them to know, in six, or eight, or ten words . . . what are those words?"

"Wow, an easy one," he said, a little thrown. "I'm going to need a minute. I work hard. So, hardworking . . . work ethic, maybe. I'm dependable, you can count on me. I'm honest, so honesty; I'm dedicated, so dedication. I get the job done no matter what . . . determination, maybe determined. I care . . . my boss always says that I score high on his 'give-a-shit' meter, so caring, I guess. I try to connect with my guys; I like being part of a team, so camaraderie, maybe. How many is that?"

"I count seven," I said: "work ethic, dependability, honesty, dedication, determination, caring, and camaraderie," I summarized. "Good job. That's a perfect list. So here's the second request. I'd like you to tell me about a situation that tends to bring out your worst, that turns you into that guy that you don't want to be but are anyway. If there is more than one situation, try to focus on the one that is most intense, or most frequent. Try to be right back in the moment; smell the smells and hear the sounds."

"Wow, another easy one," he said. After pausing, he began, "You know, it's really any situation when I feel like someone isn't committed. It's not just here with Joe, it's anywhere . . . my son's Little League team. Half the kids don't show up to practice. How are you supposed to get better as a team if only half the team shows up to practice? It's the same at my wife's job. She's a teacher. Occasionally, her alma mater will ask her to take a teacher trainee doing their practicum. Half the time, they don't show up! Here she is, trying to help them break into a new career, and they won't even help themselves by simply showing up. I don't get it. At least Joe shows up, you know. He just won't give me that one ounce more."

"So, let's talk about that, Peter," I said. "Thank you for describing those situations for me. When I first asked you to pretend you were describing yourself to a stranger, and you gave me those seven words, why do you suppose I asked you to do that?"

"I don't know," he said, reflexively. "Probably to learn what makes me tick . . . or maybe to see how I think about myself."

"Right," I said. "And what do you think those words were then?"

"The words are like my character traits," he said. "Like what a brand of something stands for."

"Exactly," I said. "You stand for those words; they're your personal brand, your personal values. And that's why I ask you about those the way I do. If I asked you to declare your personal values directly, sometimes that's too big a question and it paralyzes people. Knowing your personal values is really important for another reason, as well. Can you guess what that might be?"

"I don't know, not really . . . it just tells you what's important to me, right?"

"Yes," I replied. "It tells me what's important to you. What happens when something that is important to you is negatively impacted, like your son's teammates not showing up for practice?"

"It pisses me off," he said.

"Okay, great. That's exactly what I was looking for. Let's connect a few of the dots now." I explained personal values, triggers, and reactions as I always do. "Any of this sound familiar, Peter?"

"So, I think we both know how I react," he said.

"And how is that?" I asked, trying to be truly surprised when he told me what I already knew.

"Well, it ain't as a Victim," he said emphatically.

"And so what is it then?"

"I get angry," he said. "It's Conflict. Something's going on that I don't like, and I want to change it."

"Yes," I said. "One of your personal values has been offended, and you react. The emotion that exists, that leads to the reaction, is the energy necessary to change the thing going on that you want to change. How do you feel about the way you handle those situations?"

"It's usually not too good right away," he said. "After everyone calms down, we're usually able to figure it out."

"Why do you think it's so hard to figure it out in the moment, Peter?"

"In the moment, I'm not listening . . . I'm usually yelling or telling. I'm not interested in what anyone wants to tell me at that point. I just want it the way I want it . . . and it's usually different than the way it is."

"Do you know what an emotional hijacking is?" I questioned.

"A what?"

"An emotional hijacking," I restated.

"No, I've never heard of that before."

"The author of *Emotional Intelligence*, Daniel Goleman, talks about the idea of an emotional hijacking occurring when people are emotionally reactive. He believes that when this hijacking occurs, it shuts down the problem-solving part of the brain. It makes thinking your way out of a situation impossible. That's why when we are emotionally reactive, we are not our best selves, nor will we produce the best outcomes. It's the reason that after everyone calms down, the situation can be worked out."

"I can see that," he said. "I think that's true in my situation."

"So, let me ask you a question, Peter. What's a better situation: one where you spin up emotionally, react in Conflict, wait for everything to calm down, and then figure it out; or one where you don't emotionally react, remain solution oriented, remain your best self, and produce the best outcome?"

"Is that a trick question?" he asked. "Of course, the second one."

"Fantastic," I commended. "So, let's talk about how that works. The key to managing conflict is to understand that the emotion that exists within you, in a given situation, results because one of your personal values has been offended. Most often, the belief will be that whoever is on the other side of that situation is behaving with intent. So, for example, in Joe's case, you probably believe that Joe is intentionally not committing, meaning he's not committing on purpose, with the sole intent to antagonize you. If that were true, it would be natural for you to be angry about that. But what if that isn't true, Peter? What if Joe is simply acting on behalf of his words, his personal brand, his personal values, like you are for yours? Would you still be as angry?"

Peter was thinking about all of the things we were talking about. When he didn't have a ready answer, I continued.

"All human behavior is a function of personal values. If you don't understand someone's behavior, you don't understand their values. After talking with Joe earlier, I can confirm that he is in fact acting on behalf of his values. And it may be true that that behavior doesn't make any sense to you. But it does make sense to him, just like your behavior does to you. Joe watches the clock so closely because he has to drop off and pick up his daughter from daycare, and there isn't a moment to spare. He's a single parent now, and he is fully committed to his daughter, while doing his best to be fully committed to his job. If you understood that every time he punched out exactly on time, he was honoring his responsibility of being a parent and committed to providing a home and life for his child, would you still be as angry?"

Peter could see where this was headed now. "Of course I respect his being a parent," he said. "I have kids of my own; I completely understand the tension. It's the reason I can't work Saturdays. I have too much going on with the kids. I had no idea that dropping off and picking up his daughter was why Joe was so time conscious. I get it, it makes sense to me now."

"And how about the emotion?" I asked.

"There's no emotion . . . I understand it now," he said.

"So, what's changed then?"

"What do you mean?"

"Well, before you said his behavior pissed you off. Now you're saying that there isn't any emotion, like the anger disappeared. Did I miss something? Did Joe suddenly change his behavior?"

"No," he said.

"Okay, so what changed?" I knew the answer, but prodded Peter. "Before, Joe would punch in and punch out exactly on time. Now, Joe continues to punch in and punch out exactly on time. Before you were pissed off, now the emotion is gone. I don't get it."

"Like I said before, I understand it now," he said.

"So let me get this straight," I stressed. "Initially, you were pissed off because you believed that Joe was behaving with intent, that he was being intentionally not committed to his job; but after learning that his time sensitivity had to do with picking up and dropping off his daughter, your pissed-off-ness went away."

"That's right."

"Okay, great," I said. "That's exactly what I wanted to hear. I wanted to be sure you connected the dots between you recognizing that Joe was behaving with respect to his personal values, just like you do. His behavior has nothing to do with you, your department, or the company. If he worked somewhere else, his behavior would be exactly the same. If you didn't work here, I'd probably be having this conversation with a different manager, talking about the same thing.

Joe's behavior is about Joe," I continued. "It's got nothing whatsoever to do with you. What is about you, though, is your reaction. You were offended by Joe's behavior because that behavior offended your value of being committed. That is a hot situation for you. Any situation that you encounter where you experience someone not being committed, you will spin up. Once spun up, you will lash out. You will not be your best self, and you will not produce the best outcome. Unless, of course, you come to accept and believe that other people's behavior is simply them honoring their values.

Believing that doesn't mean you must condone, justify, accept, or practice that behavior, but if you can come to see it for what it is, them honoring their values, then nothing they do should become an emotional event in your life. When it's not an emotional event, the situation doesn't become emotionally loaded. When the situation isn't emotionally loaded, then you can remain solution oriented and pure in thought. You can always employ a third-party test, to test whether or not you are emotionally loading a situation. If I came to you today and said, 'Peter, I really need your help, man.'" I framed the situation with Peter and Joe as another manager and employee in a different dealership so that he could see it from an outside perspective. "What are some ideas that you might suggest to me, that I could bring back to that dealership in Ohio, to help them get that figured out?"

"First," he said, "they should probably have a conversation

about it. They might think about looking at the schedule. Maybe they could switch some things up to make it easier for the guy if the schedule's the problem. Maybe once they figure out what's going on, they might just leave everything alone if it's working."

"Those are some great suggestions," I said, thankfully. "Now, Peter, I'd like you to try to perceive if you feel differently about the situation in Ohio and the situation here."

"Of course," he said, almost immediately. "It's not about me there."

"Exactly," I said. "And when you can think about it that way, when it's about someone else, somewhere else; if it's different for you here, that's evidence that you are emotionally loading that situation. And that was clearly true, due to your value of commitment being offended."

REPETITION: NO INTENTION, NO EMOTION, NO REACTION

"Repetition is the mother of skill."
—Anthony Robbins

"**E**nough is enough," Steve started—even before he sat down—clearly agitated, more so than I'd ever seen in him in the past. "I told him he will never talk to me like that again. I don't need to be here, you know . . . especially if he doesn't want me here. Saturday was brutal. He was really bad in the meeting. He was mean. I've never seen anyone succeed around him that has challenged him publicly, so I usually don't engage. I had salespeople coming up to me afterward though—all day long—they couldn't believe I didn't say anything in the meeting. He was going on about Colrain this, and Colrain that. He was picking on me for acting like Kevin Colrain."

I recognized his reference to Kevin Colrain, the owner of a competing dealership, one where Jim and Steve had worked together before. Colrain had a reputation that preceded him, and Jim's comparison of Steve to him wasn't meant to be kind.

"But I couldn't let it go," he continued. "So, I talked to him alone, outside."

I asked Steve what he thought brought Jim's comments on. He said he thought they were related to a situation that he had gotten into with a customer the day prior.

"I got into it with a customer on Friday," he said.

"What happened?"

"A guy came in to pick up his vehicle, and there was a mistake in the paperwork," he recounted. "The guy flipped out. He was a major asshole. I tried to explain the situation, but the guy didn't want to hear it. He just kept saying we were fucking idiots, and he didn't understand why his company did business here. The more I tried to explain the mistake, the more he just kept saying we didn't know what the fuck we were doing. And then he made a comment about the plow we installed, and he was dead wrong about that. So, I made a point of letting him know that. There was no pleasing this guy, you know. I was trying to fix the paperwork, but we had just changed dealer management systems, and I couldn't get the printer to work. I just wanted to get the guy out of there, but I couldn't get the damn printer to work, so I couldn't fix the paperwork. It turned into a real shit show."

"What was the worst part of the situation for you?" I asked.

"He just kept saying we were fucking idiots, and we didn't know what the fuck we were doing because of the mistakes in the paperwork. I wasn't even there when they did the deal. I was off the day before—Thursday—that's when they did the deal. But they didn't spin the paperwork, they left it for me. I printed the numbers as they were on the P&S (Purchase and Sale Agreement). I guess there was some discrepancy with the numbers on the P&S, that I didn't know about . . . so it ended up wrong."

I gave it a minute before proceeding. "Steve, if you were the customer, what would you have thought about your posture?"

"What do you mean, posture?"

"I mean your manner, was it positive or negative? Were you improving the situation or making it worse?"

"Well, I wasn't making it better, that's for sure. Probably defensive."

"Were you emotional?"

"You're damn right, I was emotional," he said. "The guy was calling me a fucking idiot and kept saying I didn't know what the fuck I was doing. He's lucky I didn't fucking choke him. In the old days, I would have taken back the paperwork, torn it up in front of him, told him to get the fuck out, and 'helped' him out the door, if necessary."

"So, what stopped you?"

"The work you and I have done together," he said. "I know I can't be like that anymore."

"Is that what happened Saturday?"

"What do you mean?" he asked, confused.

"You said that you had salespeople coming up to you all day long, shocked that you didn't say anything," I reminded.

"I guess I'm getting better at not reacting."

"You're still reacting, Steve, you're just doing a better job restraining it now."

"How so?"

"If the emotion is still present, you're restraining the reaction. That's the first stage of interruption, when interrupting a reaction. The problem, though, is restraint is a diminishable resource. It's like willpower. You can run out of it. If you are faced with situation, after situation, after situation requiring restraint, at some point, you will exhaust your ability to restrain the reaction. And then you will react . . . unrestrained. A better place to be is in the second stage of interruption. That's when the emotion no longer exists. Without the emotion, there's nothing to restrain. You no longer have to worry about running out of restraint, because restraint is no longer necessary. Without the emotion, there's no energy for a reaction. No emotion, no reaction, no restraint, just a situation that you would like to be different."

"Okay, I know we've talked about this before," he said. "But, how do you *actually* do that?"

"You do that by recognizing that conflict exists when someone feels like one of their personal values has been offended." I said.

"I remember that," he began. "I guess I just need a refresher on the steps though. Do *you* really go through life, day-to-day, thinking about people and their values? If somebody pisses you off, are you thinking about what value of theirs is offended?

"Let's say you're walking by Joe's office (the owner of the dealership), and you overhear him on the phone talking about some ass-clown from the factory—meaning you—who's here to tell him how to run his business; how the guy is clueless and clearly has no idea how to run anything, let alone a car dealership."

In a former life, Steve did stand-up comedy. He had sharp wit and great timing. The way he asked me the last question, the reference to an ass-clown, had me laughing hysterically. I was trying to answer his question, but I was laughing so hard at the way he had framed it, I was literally breathless. Each time I started with a word, a burst of laughter followed. It was clear that he was amazed by my amusement. He seriously thought that I would have been offended by his characterization of me being an ass-clown.

Once calmed down, I answered his question seriously, with a question. "How often do you think about gravity?" I asked.

"About *what*?"

"Gravity."

"Gravity," he said, clearly put off. "I don't think about it at all," he said.

"Well, do you believe it exists?"

"Of course, it exists."

"How do you know?"

"I know if I slip on the ice, I'm going to fall on my ass," he said as classic comedian Steve.

"So the values thing is a little like that for me," I said. "I don't spend any more time thinking about values than you do about gravity, because I know that all human behavior is a function of one's personal values. I know others' behavior is about them, not about me. I know my reactions are about me, not others. I know I can control my own behavior and no one else's. I know conflict exists when someone feels like one of their personal values has been offended, or when one feels like another is imposing their values on them. I know certain situations will be prone to offend one's values, and in order to manage those hot situations, one must first identify them. I know that the emotion that is created when one feels one of their personal values has been offended, must be either suppressed or expressed. If suppressed, one reacts as a Victim by withdrawing, stopping communication, and feeling helpless and powerless. If expressed, one reacts in Conflict by lashing out, becoming angry and aggressive, and argumentative and combative. I know reactions create winners and losers. When we win, we win directly at the expense of another; which is simply losing in disguise, due to the creation of the harbored resentment in the loser. I know we are neither our best selves, nor do we produce the best outcomes when we are reactive. I know the only hope in managing conflict is to learn to interrupt the reaction and transform it into a response, turning the interaction from negative to positive. Seeing it simply for what it is—a situation that we would like to be different. And the only thing that matters—the only conversation that matters—is the one discussing how we would like the situation to be different, and what are we going to do about it to make it that way. Was the situation with that customer what you wanted it to be?"

"Of course not," he said. "We can't grow our business by running people out of here. I wanted the paperwork to be straight, and it wasn't. I should have looked it over more carefully."

"Why do you think that situation was so difficult for you?"

"The guy just kept saying I didn't know what I was doing," he answered. "I know how to do my job. I've been doing it for almost thirty years. I was already on edge, too."

"How so?" I asked.

"Earlier in the day, one of the guys told me that a customer had called, asking about picking up his truck a day early. When he was told that the plow installation wouldn't be done in time for that to be possible, he became a real prick, and was swearing at the salesperson. So I knew when he showed up, it probably wasn't going to be good."

"So you were primed then," I said, forgetting that that might be a reference that Steve wasn't familiar with.

"Primed? I'm not sure what that is."

"Being primed is when you've labeled a person or situation as good or bad, right or wrong, et cetera. The labels carry an emotional charge—positive or negative—priming your reaction or response. If you're anticipating a particular interaction to be bad or wrong, do you think you'll be in the same mindset and physical posture as you would be in anticipating it to be right or good?"

"Probably not," he said.

"More like, definitely not," I said. "Mindset plays a big part in this stuff. Steve, let's pretend when I got here this morning, I said, 'Hey man, I really need your help. I need you to take a ride with me to the dealership down the road.' When we arrive, the sales manager explains a situation he's struggling with. He says that a customer came in recently to take delivery of their new vehicle and noticed a mistake on the paperwork. What are some things that you might suggest to him to get this figured out?"

"First, I'd suggest they fix the paperwork," he said, matter-of-factly. "Then, in the future, I'd suggest they check it for mistakes before the customer arrives."

"Okay great," I said. "But why wouldn't you have suggested that he first assume the guy was just an asshole, nit-picking the paperwork, then suggest he go on to defend the dealership, argue with the customer, threaten to throw the customer out, and jeopardize the sale?"

"That would be absolutely ridiculous," he said, mildly annoyed.

"Yes, it would," I replied. "But it's exactly what you did."

"I guess that's right," he said.

"And why was that, Steve?"

"I let it become about me," he said.

"Let me ask you a question, Steve," I began. "If you were off on Friday—when the guy showed up to pick up his truck with the mistake on the paperwork—do you think his behavior would have been any different?"

"No, I don't think it would have been different at all," he stated assuredly.

"Okay, let's say you never worked there. Do you think his behavior would have been the same?"

"Probably the same," he said.

"What if you were never born," I asked him, pausing for emphasis. "Would the guy's behavior be the same?"

"Yes, probably the same."

"So, if the guy's behavior is the same, whether you're off or not, worked there or not, born or not, how can it be about you?"

"Yeah, I get it," he said. "It's not about me."

"*His* behavior is not about you," I said. "Your reactions *are* though. When you can think about a situation differently—like you just did—when it's somewhere else, with someone else, that's evidence that you're emotionally loading the situation when it's you, here. Was your interaction with your customer win/lose?"

"Yes," he said.

"So, you were emotionally reactive then," I assessed.

"Yes," he said. "I reacted emotionally."

"And did that make the situation better or worse?"

"Worse," he confirmed.

"And why were you reactive?"

"Because one of my personal values was offended," he answered, a little unassured.

"So, which of your personal values was offended, Steve?"

"It had to do with his questioning my ability to do my job," he said emphatically. "Saying I was a fucking idiot and didn't know what the fuck I was doing."

"And if one of his personal values was offended, Steve, and he reacted in Conflict by lashing out, how would that have sounded?"

"Probably the way it did," he said.

"Yes," I said. "Most exactly the way it did. And if we meet conflict with conflict, what do we get?"

"Uh, conflict?"

"Yes, *conflict*," I said with emphasis. "Reacting to conflict with conflict is participating in the problem. Remember when we talked about a Super Wicked Problem? Those that want to solve the problem are also causing it. They create it by participating in it. Stopping their participation is the first step toward solving the problem. With conflict though, if you don't participate in it, it can't exist. When you are emotionally reactive, you're essentially allowing the other person to control your behavior. They push your buttons, and you spin up and flip out. At that point, you're simply a puppet. And you won't be your best self, nor will you produce the best outcomes. Why on earth would you show up every day, work twelve and fourteen hours, performing at 50 or 70 percent of your ability? It doesn't make any sense to me. You are getting in your own way at that point. You owe yourself and your family your level best all day, every day. You need to perform at 95 to 100 percent of your ability to give yourself the highest probability of success, to provide the best life for yourself and your family, to inspire everyone else's performance around you. Why would you not do that?"

"No, you're right," he said. "I got in my own way."

"Perhaps that customer works in a profession where mistakes are considered inattention to detail, or carelessness. Perhaps there is some history there, that we don't know about, that carried some negative consequences to him, based on some mistake that was made. Perhaps that customer felt that the mistake was *intentional*. Was the 'mistake' in his favor or the dealership's?"

"The dealership's."

"Okay, so if there were any trust issues—meaning to say that maybe the customer doesn't really trust us, trust the fact that he got a good deal, that we were being transparent and honest—a mistake like that might make him even more suspicious, more untrusting. Of course, it wouldn't justify his reaction, calling you an idiot and saying you don't know what you're doing. But it would make it more explainable, more understandable. What do you think would change about his reaction if he truly believed that the mistake was completely unintentional, a purely honest mistake, one anyone could make?"

"I suppose his reaction might have been less intense," he surmised.

"Yes, I agree," I said. "Less intense. In order to eliminate the emotion from a reaction, it requires the offensiveness be removed from the associated behavior. If you can come to accept that all human behavior is a function of one's personal values, then whatever behavior you are witnessing is simply that person honoring their values. Now, by recognizing that, that doesn't mean the behavior is justified, condoned, or accepted; it just means it is understood for what it is. If you could have seen your customer's behavior as his acting on behalf of his values, recognizing that his behavior was about him and not about you, and seeing the situation for what it was, simply a problem to solve—like it was at the dealership down the road—how would your behavior have changed?"

"It wouldn't have been as emotional," he said, "as confrontational. I need to be smarter about this in the future."

"It *is* about getting the *smartest* outcome, Steve," I congratulated. "The smartest outcome is produced when we are able to remain solution oriented, pure in thought. The emotion hijacks the thinking part of our brain, and it makes thinking our way out of situations impossible, along with fostering reactions. That's why most often, after everyone calms down—the emotion subsides, the apologies are made, the damage done is repaired—only then are we able to problem solve. But it can be nonlinear. You can skip the whole spin-up, flip-out, do the damage, wait, and apologize, and get straight to the problem solving. And it's done by recognizing that other people's behavior is simply them honoring their values. And when you start to doubt that fact, think about someone close to you. Maybe your wife, for example. How long have you been married?"

"Almost thirty years," he said.

"Wow! Congratulations. You know how rare that is in this business. What's her name?"

"It's Linda," he replied. "And I would really like to get this figured out at home, too. We battle about things all the time."

"And we will," I said, reassuring him. "So, if I began with Linda—the way you and I did—and I asked her to pretend she was describing herself to a stranger, wanting that stranger to know everything about her that she would want them to know in six, or eight, or ten words . . . what would her words be?"

"I'm not sure how she would describe herself," he said, after giving it some thought.

"Well, how would you describe her then?"

"Kind, caring, good mother, hard worker," he said, almost all at once.

"And would you say that her behavior is in keeping with those words?" I asked him.

"Yeah, mostly," he said.

"Yesterday at 4:00 p.m., was she caring then?" I asked him.

"I can't remember specifically at 4:00 p.m.," he answered, taking the question a little too literally.

"If we called her on the phone right now, would she be caring right now?" I asked him.

"Well, she's at work," he said, being a little uncooperative. "She might not answer." He was quiet for a moment. "I still struggle with this stuff."

"I still struggle with it too," I shared. "That's natural."

"How could you possibly still struggle with this?"

"Just because I understand this stuff, doesn't make me immune to it," I said. "I'm still human. I'm not a robot. I still have moments, just fewer of them. Let's use me and my wife as an example then," I said. "Hopefully, that will make it easier for you to connect the dots. A few days ago, my wife asked me why being organized was so important to me. I told her that when things weren't organized around me, I felt like my life was out of control. And when I feel like things are out of control in my life, my nature is to change that. I equate things being out of control to my very survival being threatened, because there was a time in my life that it was. That was never true for her. She can't relate to that. For years, she just thought I was a neat freak, a product of the military. My hangers are still two-fingers apart," I said, holding up two fingers to demonstrate. "We built a big house in '03 and there are two large walk-in-closets in the master bedroom . . . both hers," I said, laughing. "They would get so full, you couldn't open the doors . . . *both* of them. It would bother me so much that when I peeked inside, my hands would shake. It would induce something like a panic attack. It was like a crazy phobia or something. I literally could not stand to be near those closets. In the early years there, after seeing that, I'd throw a massive fit, ranting and raving so loud the whole neighborhood could hear me. It's a wonder the police didn't show up," I said, exaggerating only a little.

"Wow," Steve exclaimed, looking relieved by the thought that I was nuttier than he ever was. "How did you deal with *that?*" But he didn't wait for an answer. He actually went on to answer his own question, which made my making the point for him unnecessary. *Guided self-discovery,* I was thinking. "Did you make peace with it by thinking that maybe she felt like the time she spent straightening out her closet was wasted time that she could be spending with you, or your kids—you have kids, right? —or the dog, or something . . . exercising maybe, or working more?

"Maybe it just wasn't that important to her," he speculated.

"It was different for her than it was for me," I said. "Now, I would say that her behavior is a function of her personal values, like yours or mine. And hers didn't include being organized in that way. It was a hot situation for me, because it offended my values of organization, of control, of surviving. So I lashed out," I said. "That's Conflict. And by doing so, I was essentially imposing my value of organization on her, judging her based on whether or not I believed she was honoring *my* value of being organized. Which led to me creating the behavior in her that I didn't want. And she reacted, as well, in Conflict. And we both know firsthand what conflict met with conflict leads to," I said, intentionally leaving it hanging that way.

Steve finished my sentence for me. "Conflict," he said, shaking his head in agreement.

"So, in order for us to more peacefully coexist, I needed to learn to respect the personal values of hers that were different than my own, and vice-versa. And now, better understanding those personal values, her behavior makes more sense to me; it's less offensive. It's simply a situation that I would like to be different: there is a home somewhere on planet earth, where the closets in the master bedroom are messy. What are some ideas that you might suggest to help us get this figured out?"

"Wow," he said. "When you say it that way, it's like no big deal. The lights are still on; the world didn't end." He looked out the window. "There're no riots in the streets."

"Exactly," I said. "It's just a situation. It was always *just* a situation. But I emotionally loaded the situation because one of my values was offended. I participated in the problem, I wasn't my best self, and I didn't produce the best outcome. I reacted in Conflict, I became emotional, and I was unable to think my way out of the situation. As my wife reacted to my reaction, I escalated the situation, making it worse, not better. I made it win/lose. I didn't know how to interrupt it. I felt like if I gave in, I was demonstrating *weakness* and *being vulnerable*. And that scared the shit out of me, so I overcompensated, becoming even more of a nightmare than I might have been otherwise.

"But you know what," I continued. "After all the yelling and swearing, after cleaning up the all the shit I smashed, after the tears were gone and the apologies were made, the situation still remained. There was just a problem to solve. Now, I know I could have skipped all the nonsense and gotten right to solving the problem. That would have been a better me, and produced a better outcome. Sound familiar?" I asked Steve.

"Like it happened yesterday," he said, smiling in acknowledgment. "Friday, actually."

"So as you become more adept at this, Steve, try to imagine the underlying personal value that would be driving some behavior of your wife's that might tend to spin you up. If you don't understand her personal values, you won't understand her behavior. And behavior that isn't understood can easily be interpreted as being intentionally offensive."

"But what if her personal values aren't my personal values?" he asked.

"That's the whole point, Steve. It's likely that some of them aren't. So let me ask you a question. When you described your wife in words, you said: kind, caring, good mother, and hardworking, right?"

"Yes, that's right," he said.

"Okay, Steve, please tell me which of her words—her personal values—are bad or wrong."

"It's got to be that damn 'good mother' one," he said, jokingly. "I see where you're going with this," he said. "None are bad or wrong."

"None are bad or wrong," I echoed. "And her behavior follows her personal values, just as everyone else's does, including your own. Further, if you judge her based solely on her adherence to *your* personal values, and she does the same, you both will fail to live up to each other's expectations. You'll spend your time defending your respective personal values, and the situation will remain, unchanged and unsolved. A better place to be, for the sake of your relationship—all relationships—is for each of you to learn to respect the other based on the differentness of your personal values, and learning and knowing that the behavior that results will be different as well. You may still not agree with the behavior, but at least you'll understand it. And if you can come to truly understand it for what it is—simply action or reaction on behalf of personal values—then the intentional offensiveness should subside. Without the emotion, there's no reaction. Without the reaction, there's no restraint needed. Just a situation that we would like to be different . . . a problem to be solved. And your customer on Friday, Steve . . . which of his personal values were bad or wrong?"

I knew he already knew the answer, obviously none. But in prototypical Steve fashion, as he appeared to be giving it serious thought and careful consideration, he delivered, "That customer seemed to really, really, really value the word fuck," he said. "Perhaps that, then."

"If—"

"If you can keep your head when all about you
Are losing theirs and blaming it on you,
If you can trust yourself when all men doubt you,
But make allowance for their doubting too;
If you can wait and not be tired by waiting,
Or being lied about, don't deal in lies,
Or being hated, don't give way to hating,
And yet don't look too good, not talk to wise:

If you can dream—and not make dreams your master;
If you can think—and not make thoughts you aim;
If you can meet with Triumph and Disaster
And treat those two imposters just the same;
If you can bear to hear the truth you've spoken
Twisted by knaves to make a trap for fools,
Or watch the things you gave your life to, broken,
And stoop and build 'em up with worn-out tools:

If you can make one heap of all your winnings
And risk it on one turn of pitch-and-toss,
And lose, and start again at your beginnings
And never breathe a word about your loss;
If you can force your heart and nerve and sinew
To serve your turn long after they are gone,
And so hold on when there is nothing in you
Except the Will which says to them: 'Hold on!'

If you can talk with crowds and keep your virtue,
Or walk with Kings—nor lose the common touch,
If neither foes nor loving friends can hurt you,
If all men count with you, but none too much;
If you can fill the unforgiving minute
With sixty seconds' worth of distance run,
Yours is the Earth and everything that's in it,
And—which is more—you'll be a Man, my son."

—Rudyard Kipling

RECKONING:
MY STRUGGLING WITH FAITH,
MATH, AND ABANDONMENT

"Understanding is often a prelude to forgiveness, but they are not the same, and we often forgive what we cannot understand (seeing nothing else to do) and understand what we cannot pardon."
—Mary McCarthy

"I think you need to deal with it," she said.

"I am dealing with it," I replied.

"I mean really deal with it," she said again, like I didn't hear her the first time. This time, I didn't answer. This was the hottest of hot situations for me, and I had to be in the absolute best frame of mind to have a discussion about it, or the situation could instantly spiral out of control in the worst way.

"I think you need to make peace with it," she said. And then that was it; instantly, horrifyingly, off the rails, bad. She would have been better off to have smashed me in the face with a brick, my reaction would have been gentler.

"THERE IS NO MAKING PEACE WITH IT," I thundered. "SOME THINGS ARE UNFORGIVABLE. TAKING A LIFE,

ABANDONING A CHILD . . . I'M NOT GOING TO HAVE A CONVERSATION ABOUT IT. THERE'S NO JUSTIFICATION FOR IT. THERE'S NO REASON COMPELLING ENOUGH, NO EXCUSE THAT COULD POSSIBLY BE SUFFICIENT TO CONDONE THE ACTION; IT'S GROSSLY NEGLIGENT, INEXCUSABLE, PURE SELFISHNESS, AND INCONCEIVABLY IRRESPONSIBLE. MY PARENTS HAD NO FUCKING BUSINESS HAVING A CHILD TOGETHER. MY MOTHER SHOULD HAVE HAD AN ABORTION. THAT WOULD HAVE DONE ME A FUCKING FAVOR. PEOPLE TALK ABOUT HOW TERRIBLE ABORTIONS ARE—TRY BEING AN UNWANTED CHILD— THEN LET'S HAVE THAT FUCKING CONVERSATION."

The sheer ferocity of it still surprises me. I've largely eliminated conflict from my life. I've learned to be neutral in situations that would have formerly had me shaking after venomous and vicious outbursts. But when it comes to my relationship with my father, I still boil like the sun.

"How are you going to coach people on conflict if you can't make peace with it?" she asked me. I didn't have an answer. "You're writing a book about managing conflict," she said. "People are going to have shit in their lives that they're trying to work through. They're going to want you to be able to help them. How are you going to help them if you can't work through it yourself?"

Of course, she was right . . . she had *always* been right. I wasn't making peace with it because I didn't *want* to make peace with it, not because I didn't know how. I felt like making peace with it would make what happened okay, like I was *accepting* it. I damn sure wasn't accepting it . . . EVER.

But I've learned that sometimes what, at first glance, appear to be the most conflicted situations can actually be addressed by thinking about them differently. And for my own sake, by my own reckoning, I needed to get that figured out. It may not ever mean fully making peace with it, or ever accepting it. But through some attempt of trying to understand it, and vowing never to repeat it, I may ultimately break the cycle—reducing the rage somewhat . . . still existent, though quieter.

My father turned fifty in 1992, when we reconnected. I was twenty-seven. He sent me a typewritten letter, along with his picture and a poem by Rudyard Kipling. The poem, "If—", was written in 1895, five years before my father's father was born, and published in *Rewards and Fairies* in 1910. Much like its intent when written—advice to be passed along from father to son—I suspect it was first passed along from my grandfather to my father sometime prior to the former's death in 1959. My father was sixteen when his father died, and while not the same sort or degree of separation as mine with him, it was a permanent unplanned absence nonetheless.

After our first visit—aside from the ones that took place in the first year of my life—he wrote me another long typewritten letter. At the end of it, he hand-wrote a note, saying that it sounded "harsh" when he read it . . . but he wanted me to know it wasn't intended that way. It was harsh. The letter itself was incredibly defensive, full of justifications and rationalizations, chronicling the unfairness of the circumstances, along with the wholesale diminishment of my situation . . . like he had left me with the nanny at Disney World, and my biggest struggle would be to decide which private boarding school I would attend and which house I would summer at. I think I've shown more concern for the bunny my son abandoned over ten years ago—who's become my responsibility to feed and water since—than my father did for me between the time my parents separated and the day we reconnected.

I really wasn't interested in whose fault it was. That didn't matter to me in the least. I did expect more than "things happen," though. Things fucking happen! Yes, things happen . . . you lose your car keys, you forget to pay a bill, you hit a curb and blow out a tire. Things do happen. But not—*oh yeah, now I remember . . . I got married, had a kid, disappeared for twenty-seven years, having never provided for that child's existence, and justified it by not wanting to interfere or make matters worse.* I think it's more like *I didn't want to be encumbered or responsible, tied down, limited, especially financially.* In his letter, he talks about "developing a mechanism to avoid dwelling on the pain and the frustration." He "drew a curtain," he said, "and the past no longer existed," and wrote, "I am protecting my own mental health." All I heard him saying when I read the letter was, "poor me, poor me, poor me."

My father is a smart guy. One of the smartest people I've ever met. He speaks five languages and is an electrical engineer. One doesn't need to be a rocket scientist or a Mensa candidate, though, to understand the innate, inherent, undeniable, inalienable concept that parents have a *necessarily parental responsibility* to their offspring . . . to nurture, to raise, to provide for, and to parent. It's a natural, instinctual law, for fuck's sake. Without which, any species would be doomed to extinction. Last I knew, it takes consensual parties nine months of gestation—wherein there is ample opportunity to terminate any "momentary lapse in judgement"—and a considerable amount of pain packed in to a short amount of time, birth, to remind both parents that something might require their full and undivided attention. My wife and I have dedicated every waking moment since our son was born to giving that kid a better start than we had ourselves. That's what parenting is about. And I know many—most—other people do the same.

Part of Coaching is helping people discover and connect to their life's purpose. Connecting to one's purpose focuses on tapping into, harnessing, and then deploying the incredible, sustainable power derived by identifying and pursuing one's own intrinsic and extrinsic motivations—the things that make life and work reward-ing and fulfilling. The primary difference between the extrinsic motivators (money, promotions, awards, bonuses) and intrinsic ones (love, acceptance, self-esteem, teamwork) is that the extrinsic motivators often lose their motivational qualities faster. Intrinsic motivations can drive someone for a lifetime, while extrinsic moti-vations often don't survive beyond next week's paycheck. When explaining that, I often share my own purpose—providing my son a better start in life than I had—as an example to make my point. In trying to demonstrate the power of that motivation, I'll ask: "In the course of my day, my life, what do you suppose that I would allow to get in my way of providing a better life for my son? Maybe, heavy traffic?" I'll ask them. "How about if my flight gets delayed? Maybe if it's rainy or cold outside?" There's always an extended and awkward silence that follows. Partly due to the clumsiness—and obliqueness—of my questions. I break the stillness. "Death," I tell them. Death will be the only thing that stops me from providing that kid a better life. If death stops me, it will carry on without me, if I've done my job well. It will self-perpetuate. My son will do the same for his son or daughter.

Now I'm fifty myself. My father will be seventy-four this com-ing year. We haven't spoken in a decade anyway, and I haven't seen him since we buried my mother—fifteen years, next June. My son is eighteen now. I often wonder what he would say to me if it were the two of us meeting for the first time, after a lifetime of absence and neglect. What would my letter to him sound like? Would it be defensive, full of justification and rationalization? Would it talk about how I was just a victim of circumstance? The unfairness of it all? Would I diminish his situation? Would I preserve myself at his expense? I wonder what force on earth would be strong enough to keep me from my son. And what if he had to have the same con-versation with his child when he was fifty? What would that sound like? We'd have to be experts by then, right? The explanation would have to be near perfection. Three generations of piss-poor parenting would have to have expertly crafted the message.

Like father, like son though, right? Bullshit! It's often said, in my line of work, that sons should be eternally grateful that their fathers were born first. Because it seems few sons are able to drive the business the way their fathers did. At eighteen years old now, my son is ten times the man I was at his age. He consistently outperforms his own outrageous expectations of himself, like wanting to make both the varsity tennis and football teams during his high school career; which he did, in spite of never having played football before trying out and not touching a tennis racket until he was almost thirteen years old. He aspired to go to the University of California Los Angeles, which he is attending currently; accepted to their Financial Actuarial Science program as an out-of-state student and earning both a full Army ROTC Scholarship and a full Air-Force ROTC Scholarship. And not only earning the scholarships, which in itself would have been remarkable enough, but having to first be accepted by UCLA independent of any other contributing factors, and then having the Army willing to send him there. It was his first choice school.

So was it chance? Good luck? No! He was number one in the nation in merit, so he got his first choice. He had earned it, every bit of it. Since he's been there, he's taken one of the heaviest loads of any freshman on campus, finishing his initial quarter with straight As and a B+. He's the only male freshman cadet to earn a spot on the Army ROTC Ranger Challenge Team, requiring him to be up and training at 4:00 a.m. most days. He inspires *me*! He should inspire his grandfather, because he's one thousand times the man my father was at that age. But my son's accomplishments have gone unnoticed by his grandfather, which simply adds to the list of the unforgivable.

So, where the fuck is the breakdown? On what planet is it okay to shirk your responsibility, walk the fuck away, and preserve yourself at the expense of your child? What fucking planet is that? Where do you learn that? What school do you go to? Oh, I know . . . during the instructions before takeoff, they tell you to plan your exit, use your seat cushion for flotation, and to put your oxygen mask on first, right? Before helping others . . . that must be it. The wisdom of fucking pre-flight instructions. How's this for wisdom: The thing I'm proudest of in my life is my relationship with my son. With my father, not so much. He can go fuck himself.

His letters were always addressed to me and my wife. One of the only other things I got right in my life, somehow managing to stay married to the same woman for twenty-seven years and counting. My father is somewhat of a serial spouse, however. We suspect there have been seven or eight wives over the years, but know of four for sure. My mother being the first. I also learned that I have a half-sister from a subsequent marriage. We haven't ever met, but I'm sure our discussion would be riveting. I don't know what kind of father he was to her; better, I hope. But during the times he and I saw each other, she wasn't around. He didn't talk about her much, but there was no end to the conversation about his stepchildren. I'm not sure if he was trying to impress me with his doting over them, modeling what he thought he should have done for me, or if it was simply epic tone-deafness. Like inviting a blind person to a silent movie, or an alcoholic to a wine tasting. I remember during one visit with wife-du-jour, he talked about how he had funded his stepdaughter's college fund already. How, at ten, she wanted to be a veterinarian, and he wanted to be sure to help her with that. At the time, I hadn't gone to college myself yet. I remember being absolutely astonished by the fact that he was more concerned about a stranger's kid—albeit his *now* wife's kid—than he was about his own. It felt a little like the Twilight Zone.

I was told in no uncertain terms that Burkes go to college. If I didn't attend college, I'd be the first Burke in a hundred years not to have a college degree. And he said, "The day you graduate, I'll be there." I graduated twice after that. The first with a bachelor's in accountancy and then with a master's of business administration degree. He wasn't at either one. In the big picture, it didn't matter. I didn't do it for him. I did it for me; I did it for my family. I wanted to give myself the best chance of success, the brightest future. I would have done it if he was around or not. The day *my* son graduates, though, I'll be in one of two places: at his graduation or in a casket.

When my father and I first reconnected, I owned and was running two businesses. At the time, one was growing fast. That growth created problems, putting a strain on both businesses in terms of resources: cash, manpower, my time and attention, etc. One was a local used car sales and service business and the other was a financial services business, providing a private label finance source for franchised automobile dealers to finance auto repairs. The footprint of the larger business covered forty-six states. Both were cash-intensive businesses, and when my operating account got under one hundred thousand dollars, it would send me into a tailspin. I would have a serious meltdown. It took a lot of cash to juggle the two businesses and cash was the only protection (and peace of mind) I had. Things would have to run almost perfectly to keep all the balls in the air. Inevitably, there were times when things didn't go perfectly. During one of those times, we had had a few unforeseeable setbacks. One of the dealerships I set up in California filed for bankruptcy, and the check they paid us for the initial setup bounced. Due to the bankruptcy, we knew chasing payment was futile. We had a car stolen that was sold, and one totaled after someone crashed through our dealership's front line. Of course we had insurance, but with cash flow, timing is everything. I was running out of cash, worried about making payroll, and I felt panicked—one of the few times in my life—and allowed myself to be victimized by it. In that moment, I was paralyzed by fear, becoming physically short of breath and catastrophizing. Imagining everything I'd worked for blowing up and failing everyone that had believed in and supported me, putting everything they'd entrusted to me at risk.

As I always do in a crisis, I called my wife. She was at school. Trying to maintain my composure but breaking down, I told her we were running out of money, and I didn't know what to do. I was completely overwhelmed. My senses were dulled, my body was limp, my mind was blunted, time seemed to slow. She said she was going to call my father. I didn't have the energy to object. The fight, at that point, was out of me. A couple of days later, we had a check for $20,000. When we talked, he said that it was for a lifetime of birthdays and Christmases missed, along with those in the future. When he and my wife talked, he told her that he just wanted my life to be better. I was grateful for his help. We put the cash in the bank, and never touched it . . . to this day. Fortunately, it never got to that point, although perilously close. That was the one and only time he's helped me in my life.

A few years later, my mother died. She had managed to save a fair amount of cash along with her house and car that were paid for. I was the only heir, so I had a substantial windfall. Over the years, I had become joint-tenants in the house, the car, and the bank accounts, so the transition after her death was pretty seamless. We buried my mother on my son's fourth birthday. My father came up for the funeral to "support me," bringing his then-wife and her daughter, my so-called sister. That was the last time I saw him, June 15th, 2001 . . . almost fifteen years ago now. During our last phone conversation, he asked me to repay him the money he had sent me. Saying he could use it, speculating that with the money I'd gotten from my mother, I didn't really need it anyway. Surprised, I said, "Sure, I can do that."

I asked my wife to get a cashier's check for $20,000 payable to him. She got the check made, and we were getting ready to mail it out.

"I want you to know I don't agree with this," she said.

"Agree with what?" I asked her.

"Sending the money back. It's your money, and it's your father, so you do what you want. But I think it's bullshit."

"What's bullshit about it?"

"The guy has done nothing for you your whole life," she said. "The one time he does something for you, he wants it back now. No. Fuck off. We've spent more than $20,000 on our kid, every year of our kid's life. Try being a fucking parent."

Sometimes when my wife feels like I'm not sticking up for myself, she wants to defend me. It was clearly the case here. But what she said was true. Aside from a couple weeks' time in total, over about an eight-year period, there was no evidence that I existed in his life. And while incredibly selfish on my part, I didn't return the money, because I wanted it—me—to cost him something. At least then, I thought, he'd have twenty thousand more reasons to think about me. I never met my father's father or my father's mother, one dying before I was born and the other just as my father and I were re-uniting. My sense is, though, they invested a lot more in him than he ever did in me.

I wrote earlier: I've learned that sometimes what, at first glance, appear to be the most conflicted situations can actually be addressed by thinking about them differently . . . and for my own sake, by my own reckoning, I needed to get that figured out. This—my father and I—was clearly one of those. It wasn't the only, big, messy problem I'd struggled with. The first big, messy problem was one between me and God.

Like many people, I believed in God because that's what I was taught. I was baptized Catholic, and after my mother was made unwelcome in the Catholic church, I finished my other sacraments as a Lutheran. I attended Sunday School and rarely missed a service. For me, believing in God was no different than believing in Santa Claus, the Tooth Fairy, or the Easter Bunny. The toughest of those, for me, was Santa Claus. Delivering gifts worldwide in a single night, down each chimney, etc., didn't work for me. The logistics didn't add up. I was always a Santa Claus skeptic. The God question though . . . that was late in coming.

For me, belief in a religion, or God, is a very personal thing. We each have had experiences in life that would lean us toward one conclusion or another. I'm no different; I've had a number of those experiences. It's those experiences that have made my conceptual struggle with the idea of God so incredibly difficult to reconcile. For example: surviving an accident in a car that had flipped over several times—estimated flipping at 80 miles per hour—on the lawn of a Methodist Church in the wee hours of Easter Sunday. The emergency professionals who responded on the scene expected deceased occupants. They were amazed by the fact that there were no fatalities. Was it luck? Was it just good automotive engineering? Was it divine intervention? I didn't know about any of that. I just knew it was a serious crash that I survived. But did that minimize it then? If I didn't acknowledge the obvious symbolism, was I being callow or contemptuous?

When I was young, probably seven or eight, I had a dream one night. It's one of two dreams in my life I'll never forget. It was quick. I remember a blinding white light, like from a flash-bang grenade or lightning. And a single word, spoken like thunder: "LEADER." That's it. And I don't think I imagined it. The message never seemed to manifest in my life though . . . almost like a fax sent to the wrong number, or spam in your inbox. Maybe I wasn't the intended recipient. But it had a strange, residual quality, unlike dreams I'd had before. Was it a message, a hallucination? Perhaps, the television was left on, and I heard the word in between waking and sleeping. I don't know what it was, and maybe never will.

The second dream was the opposite of that and probably thirty years later. This one was terrifying. The dream itself took place in complete and absolute blackness, but there was a presence. A malignant, deleterious, and threatening presence. No shape, really, and featureless, but pervasive and intimidating in its manner. "HAVE YOU HAD ENOUGH YET?" That's what it asked me. The voice wasn't thunderous, like the previous dream. It was more like a synthesized voice; the kind you'd hear when someone who's being interviewed on *60 Minutes* is hiding their identity. And after the question, I remember screaming angrily, "NO. I HAVEN'T HAD E-FUCKING-NOUGH YET!" Then I remember commencing to fight against whatever it was with all my might. Like in the movie *Divergent*, when Tris or Four completed a test in one of the simulations, the entity simply deconstructed and vanished. I don't know what that was. I do know that following that, for a period of many years, until I found coaching, was the worst stage in my life. I've lived a life with no shortage of challenges. So, I wonder, was I not paying close enough attention to something? Was I in some sort of denial? An old friend of mine once told me that if God is trying to send you a message, "Listen for the whisper, or watch out for the brick." Perhaps, I hadn't heard the whisper.

I attended a Catholic college in my thirties, and during my undergrad, I took the required twenty-four credits of philosophy and religion. For most secular programs, that would have qualified as a minor. Suffice it to say, I learned a great deal about philosophy and religion. In the grad school's MBA program, I concentrated in finance. The more I learned about diversifying stock portfolio's, managing risk, Black–Scholes Capital Asset Pricing Model, the less appetite I had for that risk. Instead of being more comfortable with it, by virtue of familiarization, I was less so. That was true for me as well, with respect to the concept of religion, God, and the Church.

Looking back, I guess I would say I had a crisis of faith. I came to see the Church as a business, simply selling salvation and monetizing the Word. I was home one day, and the doorbell rang. I answered the door, and it was a Jehovah's Witness, inviting me to join them in celebrating their faith. He introduced himself to me, and he asked me what I believed in. Reflexively, I said, "Education. I believe in education." For years afterward, I struggled with the idea of believing in God. The sticking point, for me, was: Does God exist? It's not my nature to be blindly faithful, or obedient. So I was stuck in this endless loop, struggling with a decision contingent on the answer to the unanswerable. Einstein said that the definition of insanity is doing the same thing over and over, expecting a different result. I think seeking to prove something unprovable is a little like that also. It was then that I decided to stop asking does God exist and start asking whether one's belief in God benefits those individuals and humanity. Now, regardless of God's actual existence, we have an answerable question, with evidence that can either support or refute that position. The benefits to individuals and society as a whole can be measured and proven, or disproven. If the benefits outweigh the consequences, then belief in God is justified, productive, and good.

One component of coaching is wanting a little bit more for the person you're coaching than they want for themselves. Seeing what they can become, not what they are. Inspiring them to reach beyond themselves to achieve things they once thought unachievable; to lift them up, to help them in identifying and breaking through the things that are limiting them in life, and helping them gain the courage to do that. I think God is like that for people. If that's really true for those people, then belief in Him is beneficial for them, regardless of His actual existence. As such, I view the Church's role differently now, recognizing that it must sustain itself to continue to support its quest, to cultivate faith. Faith, which I believe—all things considered—ultimately benefits humanity. So the lesson for me was in learning to approach problems differently, seeking a solution by changing the nature of the problem and my perspective.

The next big, messy problem—a math problem—was one of blending disparate variables. While in the MBA program, I decided to build a statistical model that could measure a given employee's entire performance based on a set of key performance indicators—vetted to positively correlate with an organization's definition of individual success—collapsed into a single number. Let's say we had a thousand employees, each being measured on their total sales in dollars, profit margin by percentage of sales, the number of repeat and referral clients, customer satisfaction measured as an index, number of units shipped, number of cancelled orders, number of days absent, timeliness of expense reports, etc. I wanted to be able to communicate that cumulative score for each employee in a single number. The challenge, then, was to figure out how to blend the disparate units of measure.

I struggled with that for over two years. Finally, I realized that I couldn't combine the disparate units of measure directly, but I could combine something they shared in common . . . their relative position to each other and to the mean within the distribution. With a distributed performance, I could simply sum the individual standardized numbers. For instance: each individual's performance (χ) averaged together, becomes the mean performance (μ) of that attribute. Then, the average distance between all of the individual points on the distributed curve, divided into that mean performance, becomes the standard deviation (σ). And when determining the distance of any individual performance, minus the mean, divided by the standard deviation, yields a standardized number (Z). The standardized number indicates how far a particular individual's performance is from the mean in the unit of a standard deviation, which done for everyone is then additive. So, that means that one could end up with a single number representing an employee's entire relative performance over a number of disparate—and formerly un-combinable—units of measure. An Employee Performance Measurement index, as I called it.

Why is that worthwhile to think about? Think about what's going on in the world today. Terrorism. It has absolutely consumed the media. Any mention of focusing on a particular segment of the population as a possible countermeasure is met with utter disgust and labeled profiling. In the age of Big Data, you don't need to profile people, you can pinpoint and isolate people's behavior. In this case, the person's attributes are the lagging indicators, and their behaviors are the leading indicators. Let's use the former example of measuring an employee's performance. If we determined that the employee with the highest sales in dollars, combined with the highest profitability as a percentage of sales, combined with the highest number of repeat and referral clients, combined with the highest customer satisfaction index score, combined with the highest number of units shipped, combined with the lowest cancellation rates, combined with the lowest absenteeism, combined with the speediest filing of reports, was most valuable employee to the company, then the person with the highest cumulative standardized number would be that person. Nothing else about them would be relevant, or measured, or known for that matter (i.e., race, gender, religion, sexual orientation, right or left-handedness, hair or eye color, IQ). It's purely an indicator of what the company considers optimum performance by an employee based on the key performance indicators that were selected. Likewise, let's say as a nation we determined that those same items in the former example represented the key performance indicators of a terrorist's behavior. If that were true, then we should necessarily focus on the individual with the highest standardized number, regardless of race, gender, religion, sexual orientation, right or left-handedness, hair or eye color, IQ, because that would indicate the highest cumulative probability of terroristic behavior.

Unfortunately, it's likely in the future that everyone will have to have some type of a Terrorism Threat Index Score. And it will be based on the cumulative probability of key performance indicators, those determined to be positively correlated with terrorist acts. That aside, regardless of its usefulness, blending the disparate variables required changing the problem's nature, and again, my perspective.

So, back to the big, messy problem of me and my father. Most problems become intractable because we get caught up in a Super Wicked Problem: those who want to solve the problem are also causing it. We are unable or unwilling to see a point of view different than our own, and as such, we continue participating, in spite of knowing we should stop. We become driven and blinded by emotion. That's true of any of the big problems in our society, e.g., capital punishment, abortion, gay rights, racism, religion, or adultery, etc. I can't dispassionately think about my abandonment. I couldn't then, and I can't now. I will go to my grave not accepting his behavior. Many people can't do that with abortion or capital punishment, gay rights, or whatever else. So the problems remain, because a value of theirs was offended by a situation that exists, that challenges how they see the world and everything in it. They spin up emotionally and withdraw or lash out, creating the behavior in others that they don't want. It becomes a self-fulfilling cycle that's difficult to break, reinforced with each revolution, by metaphorical, centrifugal force. A chain of reactions, each reaction exacerbating the other.

So, as a trained professional and an expert in managing conflict, I can only employ the approach that I believe to be effective at breaking that cycle. That is, recognizing that my father's behavior was simply a function of his personal values: maybe fairness, self-protection, survival, or freedom, for example. He experienced some situation that challenged one (or more) of those values. Maybe an argument (or worse) with my mother, maybe the contemplation of a failed marriage, or becoming a parent at too early an age. Then he reacted as a Victim, by fleeing. And maybe that's why it's so impossible for me to comprehend, because my nature is to fight, despite any odds, not flee. No doubt, fighting would have caused its own aftermath, no better certainly, only different. But I would more easily understand the fighting, because I'll never understand the fleeing. Perhaps that's why I find the letters to be so shamelessly self-serving, and his defensiveness so galling, because it embraces that which I rebel most strongly against. But in the most unimaginably ironic and tragic way, he did victimize me, by first becoming a victim himself. Perpetuating it. Doing to others what was done to him. And likewise, I chose Conflict. Never wanting to be a victim again, I fought . . . doing to others what was done to me. How heartbreaking, for both of us. We are the same, yet different. Two sides of the same coin. But I have changed my nature. I can live with myself now. He hasn't changed his, and I don't know how he lives with himself.

For years, I've punished myself and everyone else around me

for my abandonment. Think about how absolutely insane, and counterintuitive, that is. But, I did it anyway. I believed that I wasn't good enough for my father to want to stick around and parent me. I believed that the choice he made, to leave, was about me. Then I think about how I feel about my own son. How he's given my life meaning and purpose, and how blessed I am that he and my wife continued to love me when I was at my absolute worst . . . and I punished *them* for *my* abandonment. The day my wife said that she and my son were afraid of me, because I was so explosive, was the day it all changed for me. That day I knew it had to be different.

Change is a function of increased self-awareness and awareness of others. The most difficult and protracted cases of persistent conflict that I deal with exist with people whose behavior has no consequence to them. For many years, that was true for me . . . until it wasn't. Then, in a spectacular display of hitting the wall like a wind-up toy, I bounced off and continued to hit it over and over again, until the wall broke me, and then change was possible. My father is able to continue to behave the way he does because there have been no consequences to him for his actions. Sure, he might have missed the money he sent me, but aside from that, nothing. So my expecting his future behavior to change, without the consequences necessary to force that change, is a little nutty on my part as well. I've made peace with the future not changing. I've made peace with the fact that he isn't part of my life, or my son's life. I'll never make peace with the past though.

I often think about the absurdity of us sharing a name. I'm the fourth Richard, but the first Richard William—my father's ineffectual attempt at giving me my own identity. The first rule in marketing a product re-launch (a product which initially failed in the marketplace and is being readied to be reintroduced) is to completely change the product's name. A wholesale re-branding. My son's name isn't Richard on purpose; I don't expect his son's will be either. In fact, my son's name begins with the letter of the alphabet that is furthest away from the letter R.

On the cover of this book, you'll notice I've referenced myself as R. W. Burke. While I would have loved to fully change my name— and I've often thought of publishing this under a pseudonym—I wanted to avoid all the legal complications that would result. Instead, I resorted to disaffiliation, dissociation, and disempowering the label and the reminder. So R then. And R can stand for: Reflection, Readiness, Rage, Reality, Reason, Responsibility, Realize, Recurrence, Reaction, Rampage, Refrain, Repetition, Reckoning, Response, and Resolve . . . anything but Richard.

When I finish writing this book, I will be done with him forever. He will not be given another thought, because he hasn't earned it and doesn't deserve it. He is dead to me. You can't resolve conflict with another human being if they don't participate in the resolution. It's not a one-way street. And if these are the last words he reads or hears from me before his true passing, I'm okay with that . . . that, I've made peace with.

RESPONSE:
COACHING YOURSELF UP

"Fire cannot quench fire. Water does."
—L. E. Farase

My wife was crying. "Is this how you coach people?" she asked, with indictment. "You yell at them? How is that supposed to help anybody? You suck as a Coach."

I remained perfectly quiet. She was upset about a situation that she had created for herself. When she became stuck in that situation, dissatisfied with it but doing nothing about it, I suggested she take control of it. She was allowing herself to be victimized by the circumstance, and I was becoming increasingly frustrated by her inability or desire to take command of it.

Well, that would be the storybook version of it. What I really said, after spinning up in a way that was reminiscent of the past, was, "TAKE CONTROL OF YOUR FUCKING LIFE." Nothing brings back the fuck-you guy in me like feeling stuck in a situation, helpless and powerless to do anything about it, nakedly subject to the whims and inclinations of others who clearly have their best interests in mind, not mine. I was rebelling against that, for her.

That rebellion was filled with boundless, unquenchable fury and rage, still on call after being victimized myself by an offense a half-century ago.

Every Friday or Saturday night, we go to dinner. It's our routine. I'm away from home two hundred nights a year, so it's a chance to reconnect and unwind. Since my son was born, each Friday or Saturday night, he would stay with his maternal grandmother, providing for our date night. During dinner one of those nights, my wife was telling me a story about a meeting she attended at her new school. For the last dozen years or so, she had been teaching at an inner-city charter school, and she was worried that the school's charter might not get renewed. The school was in some fiscal difficulty, and the math test scores were unacceptable. So, she decided to explore some other opportunities within the district. She was able to locate an opening for a suitable position at one of the larger high schools in the area. She would be leaving a school with two hundred kids and transitioning to a school with two thousand. The teaching staff was ten times larger than her previous school also, from her previous twenty-teacher cadre to over two hundred. As such, there were additional layers of positions: teachers, leads (lead teachers), department heads, and administration. I always worry about the safety of the schools and the working conditions for her, but she said that the school had a satellite police station inside it, and the facility was state of the art. She was most excited about the upgrade in facility, making the days there more bearable.

I've not always agreed with the moves she's made in her professional life, but she has always proved me wrong. She has the uncanny ability to make exactly the right move at exactly the right time. Something I've always envied, because I seemed to have mastered exactly the opposite of that. Weeks prior to her taking the position, though, I did sense some trepidation on her part. She had attended a required workshop over the summer, which allowed her to meet some of the fellow faculty members. The reception she received was pretty frosty, particularly from a teacher who had been teaching an advanced English class that my wife was now responsible for, and the lead teacher . . . turns out they were buddies. It also turns out that her trepidations were well founded.

So, she arrives at this meeting. The lead teacher is taking attendance. When he gets to my wife, he says, "Burke" as he's checking his roster. After recognizing her presence and pausing a moment, he continues with, "You're not a B-u-r-k-e, you're a B-u-r-k," followed by a giggle. "Do you know what that means?"

My wife, half paying attention and not wanting to give any potentially derogatory comment additional life, replied with a quick, "Of course I know what that is," to move the conversation along, not really knowing its intended meaning. So as she was telling me the story, I searched "burk" online. According to one online dictionary, burk can mean a nob, a fool, a stupid person, or an idiot. But as I was reading additional usages at some other online listings, I learned that it is also a slang term for *cunt*. When I showed her that, she was shocked. And rightfully so. Any of the references to her name were inappropriate. It was her married name anyway; it was really my name the guy was talking about. I told her she should file a formal complaint, and that I didn't want her to go back. I felt that the guy was clearly unprofessional, and should be removed from his lead position.

The more I thought about it, the more the old me started to emerge, albeit only for a split second, but it's still never a good thing. The old me imagined paying the school a visit, dragging that motherfucker out of his classroom in the middle of the day, beating him to within an inch of his life and roasting his ass on the burning inferno that would have been his car, moments after I set it ablaze. Hoping afterward, he'd remember that there are few things worse than bullying women, even if only with some word he'd learned playing Scrabble, sitting in his one-room apartment without the view, cooking up canned meat and cheese macaroni, while tending to his fish.

Then she told me about his sidekick. These guys always have sidekicks. His sidekick was a fellow teacher who had been displaced in teaching a particular class by my wife, who was eminently more qualified. Her taking over that class was most of the reason she was hired to begin with. As such, with him feeling slighted, he repeatedly tried to intimidate her with his physicality, like our St. Bernards, who quickly learn how to use their size and weight to move people or objects based on whatever it is at the moment that's seized their attention. She said that her conversations with him were always tense, and his posture was mildly menacing.

Probably the only fortunate byproduct of living with me for almost thirty years is that she isn't easily frightened, so in spite of his efforts to be imposing, in reality, he simply appeared pathetically lacking. Despite that, though, my mind immediately went to thoughts of breaking people's bodies. *Elbows and knees,* I thought. The most effective way to break people is attacking elbows and knees and, in turn, using elbows and knees as weapons. In my mind, I imagined deploying a devastating knife-edge kick to the knee of that sack of shit, followed by an elbow smash to the jaw, enjoying the view of the look in his eye and the pain on his face, as he lay crumpled in a pile on the pavement, pissing himself, wondering what just happened.

Oblivious of my amazement that two grown men with body mass indices larger than their IQs—and probably over five-hundred pounds of poorly distributed dead weight between them— would be so threatened and confrontational with a one-hundred-pound woman, and she continued to tell me about the lack of responsiveness on behalf of the administration. How she believes that they just want the situation to "go away." How the union representative is absolutely useless, even less than useless, an actual impediment to resolving the situation. How the head of the city's Human Resources Department is also the city solicitor, on the one hand, wanting to thoroughly investigate the situation and protect an employee from workplace bullying and harassment, but simultaneously wanting to settle a dispute and get a faculty member back to work.

As I'm listening, I'm imagining someone playing a game of chess with themselves, spinning the board around between moves, trying to remain independently focused and immune to the knowledge and influence of prior moves between future moves. Then a stray thought emerges: how she offered to be transferred back to her previous school, where a suitable opportunity existed, based on their need of a specific qualification she uniquely possessed, and how the school district refused to act. In that way, they were perpetuating an already prolonged unaddressed situation with a ready solution, for no apparent reason beyond intransigence. The situation was starting to negatively impact her health, evidenced by dangerously high blood pressure, which now needed to be continuously monitored by a physician and moderated with prescribed medication. It was all too much for her . . . and me. I was overwhelmed with her hopelessness and despair. And that's when the words were released: "TAKE CONTROL OF YOUR FUCKING LIFE."

Part of her shock and inability to navigate the situation was due to her never having faced anything similar in the past. Her choices professionally were unquestionably sound, unassailable. Given that, she was paralyzed by the surprise of a failed decision, and immobilized by the sheer intractability of the predicament itself. Now, lacking the confidence to make any move whatsoever, trapped in a way suggestive of Seligman's learned helplessness. My words, then harsh, moved her forward from the present to the future; one of the primary responsibilities of any capable coach.

Of course, not in the same way that any other ordinary coaching engagement would have taken place, given my emotional investment, but the way it did nonetheless. As we talked about it more calmly, she asked me how I could say such a thing. And I simply explained that sometimes people need to be "punched in the mouth," hyperbolically speaking. That non-literal reference coming to represent one being challenged to rise up to defend oneself; to transition from being victimized by a situation to being willing to end the victimization. To get angry, to intercede, to stop the harm, to end the suffering, to simply say: no more. We didn't talk about it again for a while. But the next time we did, she thanked me for helping move her forward. She realized that she had been playing into the victim role, accepting the seeming insolvability of the situation as truth.

After thanking me for helping her snap out of out what was keeping her mired in self-pity and blame, she explained that she had gotten angry about it. Incensed at the circumstance, indignant of the lack of support and assistance she had been receiving, and furious at the revolting behavior patently condoned, but then suddenly recognizing that this was her situation and only hers to solve. She had made a plan to work her way out of that situation, and in the meantime would make the most and best use of the time she had available as a result, coming to see a most unfortunate circumstance as more of a blessing in disguise.

In iPEC terms, she had shifted. She had worked her way through the energetic levels of Victim, Conflict, and then Responsibility. Each level was healthier for her, with respect to her existence, than the former. She had successfully transformed her negative reaction into a positive response, in turn, transforming a negative situation into a positive one. She had coached herself up in a way that I was proud of.

Converting a reaction into a response requires an element of self-responsibility. That's simply the willingness to take ownership of one's own behavior: forgetting about the blame and the focus on whose fault it was, extinguishing the anger and the need for dominance or retribution, and fully accepting and understanding that in whatever the situation is the solution to it lies within oneself. Sometimes, you have to coach yourself up.

It's an ongoing process. Even for me, it's a process. Like an addict would say "once an addict, always an addict," I am, in that sense, always an addict. I have to continuously monitor myself, with respect to my reactiveness. No matter how much less reactive I've become, there are still moments I'm not proud of. There are still moments in which I have to coach myself up.

Case in point, my schedule is pretty nuts. I usually have zero margin for travel mishaps. It's not uncommon for me to be booked a year in advance, so any travel interruption can ripple through a year's worth of destinations and appointments. One morning, I was headed to Wilbraham, MA. I had stayed in a hotel in Springfield, MA, the night before, so I was pretty close by. My commute was about fifteen minutes, depending on traffic and the route I chose. After packing up and leaving the hotel, I was stopped at a red light, so I checked my email. I saw an urgent message from the airline I was booked on later that evening. I was scheduled to fly from Hartford to Philadelphia for work in South Jersey the next day. The email said that the flight had been cancelled. As soon as my eyes left the screen, my energy—energetic level—plunged. I immediately reacted as a Victim, and called my wife. She's the only one that will listen to me complain, and she's heard it a thousand times over the years, due to my having spent lots of years working on the road.

"My flight's cancelled," I said.

"Why?"

"I don't know. It didn't give a reason."

"What now?" she asked me.

Then the Victim reaction flooded in. "Don't they understand how busy I am?" I vented. "I can't have flights cancelled, it causes a nightmare in my schedule. Now, I'm going to have to spend the day trying to get this figured out. And I have a meeting in twenty minutes. I'm never going to have enough time to fix this. I'm going to be busy all day."

"Why don't you drive?" she suggested.

"Not enough time," I said. "I've already rented a car in Philly. I booked a hotel based on arriving in Philly, so, if I don't fly to Philly, I'll have a car I don't need rented and a hotel booked I won't need to stay at."

"Well, let me know if you need me to do anything," she said, before hanging up, knowing that having a conversation with me when I'm in this mode is pointless. No solution would work at that time, and I wasn't ready to let it. Then I shifted to Conflict. "That airline sucks. The people there are fucking useless. Traveling by air is so fucking unreliable. I'm never going to fly that airline again. Half my flights are either delayed or cancelled, it's so fucking ridiculous. I shouldn't have to deal with this shit. You'd think someone from the airline would be on the phone right now, trying to get me re-booked. They fucking suck."

Then I shifted to Responsibility. "Okay, this is what I signed up for. Traveling is part of it. The work is rewarding and fulfilling, it's amazing. Traveling sucks no matter what, so at least the work makes it worth the pain. I have a job to do in ten minutes. The people there deserve my best. I can't be my best if I am in these modes. I need to push the reset here, get my head straight, so when I hit the door, I'm me at my best. I'll get this travel situation figured out during lunch, or I'll call the corporate travel desk; that's what they're there for. They'll help me get it worked out. I'll fly from Providence in the morning; that will get me one night at home, and I'll keep the hotel and car reservations, but change the dates, which I'm sure they'll accommodate, given my flight cancellation."

Then I shifted to Concern. "I owe my best to the people I'm working with today. If I'm focused on my own issues, I can't be fully present and focused on theirs. That's not fair to them. I need to be better than that for them. I'm sure the people at the airline are getting hammered right now. Of course, they don't want these cancellations any more than passengers do. It interrupts operations and impedes their ability to make money. The weather is beautiful, so it must be crew or mechanical. Probably a last minute issue."

Then a final shift to Reconciliation, as my phone was ringing.

"Hello," I answered.

"Mr. Burke, this is Melanie, from the ABC Airlines. I'd like to try to get you re-booked. Your flight out of Hartford for this evening was cancelled. Do you still need to get to Philadelphia tonight?"

"I'd like to catch the 6: a.m. out of Providence tomorrow morning," I said.

"Let me see what's available," she said. "Will it be the same return date?"

"The return date is the same," I said, "early Saturday, I believe."

"I have a roundtrip scheduled in between, from Philly to Long Island MacArthur, and back." After a few more moments holding, she came back and asked, "Do you prefer a window or an aisle?"

"An aisle," I replied.

"Okay, then," she said, "I have you re-booked on the 6:00 a.m. flight from Providence to Philly tomorrow morning, returning Saturday at 8:00 a.m. Does that sound right?"

"Sure does," I said. "Thanks for your help. I appreciate you being proactive about this," I said.

"And we appreciate your patience," she replied.

As I was hanging up, I was pulling into the parking lot of the dealership I was scheduled to be working at that day. That entire episode took less than fifteen minutes. I had experienced a situation that offended my values. My flight was cancelled. It offended my value of delivering on the commitment I made to the dealership I was scheduled to be working with in South New Jersey the following day. I initially reacted as a Victim, feeling helpless and powerless, not interested in anyone's helping me or helping myself. Then in Conflict, pissed off at the airline, at the airline's employees, at the need to be reliant on that form of transportation, at the world really. Finally, coaching myself up to Responsibility, and then Concern, and finally, Reconciliation. Ultimately, the problem was solved. But I could have solved it sooner, and with much less drama, if I was able to skip the negative reactions and simply see the situation for what it was: a cancelled flight. I do this routinely with people. When I witness another's behavior, I remind myself that their behavior is about them; it's not about me. I know they are simply honoring their values, whether I agree with those values or not. I try to see the situation as a problem to be solved, which requires my best self and the best outcome. As I tell my Coachees, "Work with people is never done." Clearly, I still have more work to do on me.

STEP FIVE—
CRAFTING A RESPONSE

―――――

"Between stimulus and response, there is a space.
In that space is the power to choose our response.
In our response lies our growth and freedom."
—Viktor E. Frankl

"I see it completely differently now," Gary said, after we'd talked a while.

"How so?" I asked him.

"Because it isn't his fault," he said, talking about the situation he'd described to me earlier. One where he'd become so spun up, he'd wanted to flip his desk over. When I asked him more about that situation, he explained that it was because he thought that one of the salespeople was being stupid and naive. Of course, immediately, I knew that that was simply his reaction, in Conflict, to one of his personal values being offended, but we hadn't gotten there yet.

I was meeting with Gary to follow up on our previous conversation of a couple of months ago. He was explaining some of his recent challenges, those he faced with respect to being what he described as "hot tempered." I asked him if he ever felt like that part of him got in his way. He said he believed it did, and said he felt that it held him back. I told him that I believe many people hold themselves back personally and professionally, based on their inability to get along with others. If instead, he could become known for building people up, rather than tearing them down, there would be no limit to his opportunity or success in the future.

I asked Gary my usual set of questions. "Oh boy," he said instantly. Then, after a brief pause, gave the following values: driven, honest, fair, passionate, and aggressive.

"Great," I said. "That's a perfect list to begin with. Next, I'd like you to tell me about a situation that tends to bring out your worst, that turns you into that person that you don't want to be but are anyway."

"Wow, these are tough," he said. "It's really any situation that doesn't go the way I want it to." As we were talking, he brought up a more specific situation that had happened just that morning. "Just this morning," he began, "I was working with Evan. Evan was working with the Sales Desk, trying to close a deal and asking me for interest rates. I had overheard some of the conversation between him and his customer, and him and the manager at the Sales Desk. The customer was telling him something that I believed to be untrue, and I thought Evan should have doubted its truth as well. But he wasn't even challenging the customer, he was just taking what the customer said as gospel. Then he wants the dealership to drop its drawers, selling a vehicle short that we can't easily replace, all because he doesn't have the balls or the smarts to understand what's going on."

As he continued, the intensity of his mannerisms and volume of his voice increased. "And the desk was playing along, because they are too fucking lazy to get off their asses to go talk to a customer. I told him, 'You are a fucking idiot. The guy can't possibly do what he's telling you he can do. Don't play his game. Don't be a stupid fucking asshole. Get the fuck out of my office and don't come back until you get your head out of your ass. And don't think for a minute, I'm going to set up financing for that fucking deal.' I wanted to flip my fucking desk over. I was ready to kill somebody. I was like, 'Fuck you and fuck you,'" he said, as he was holding up the middle fingers on both hands, motioning to the imaginary salesperson and desk manager.

"Ok, great," I said. "That's a great example of a situation that brings out your worst. Thank you for sharing that with me. I mentioned earlier that I would connect the dots for you as we went along. Now that we have your words and your situation, we can begin to tie this all together. When I asked you to pretend you were describing yourself to a stranger, what you were really doing was declaring your personal values. Identifying personal values is critical, because all human behavior is a function of one's personal values. If I followed you around long enough, I could tell *you* what your values are . . . you wouldn't have to tell me." I paused for emphasis. "They manifest in your behavior. When you identify your personal values, you are also identifying your triggers," I instructed. "Conflict exists when someone feels like one of their personal values has been offended. When someone feels like one of their personal values has been offended, they will spin up emotionally and react. Can you relate to that, Gary?"

"Absolutely," he said. "It's like a flash-bang."

"In what way?" I probed.

"Well, you know, one minute I'll be part of a situation that's not going the way I want it to, and then that's when the flash-bang thing happens. It's like lightning and thunder. The lightning is me getting all charged up by the situation, and then the thunder is the explosion that follows," he clarified.

"That's a great way to describe it, Gary," I congratulated. "When someone feels like one of their personal values has been offended, they will become emotionally charged," I started. "That emotion must be suppressed or expressed. If it is suppressed, the reaction will be as a Victim. That person will withdraw, stop communicating, and feel helpless and powerless. The prevailing idea will be 'I lose,'" I proceeded. "Or, if the emotion is expressed, the reaction will be in Conflict. That person will lash out, become angry and aggressive, argumentative and combative, and the prevailing idea will be 'I win.' When we are reactive, we are not our best selves, nor do we produce the best outcomes. Reactions create winners and losers; we make ourselves losers if we react as a Victim, or others losers if we react in Conflict. And while you may win in a particular situation, by reacting in Conflict, winning becomes the same as losing, because you will be winning directly at the expense of the other party. Simply inviting that behavior in them, whenever the next opportunity to return the favor presents itself. Sometimes, we create the behavior in others that we don't want. And it's often a byproduct of our own behavior."

"Okay, I get that," he said.

"So the biggest challenge in all of this is to learn how to interrupt that negative reaction, and then transform it into a positive response," I dared. "It still allows you to win in a situation, but you don't have to do it directly at the other person's expense. It's a response that you would be proud of, one as your best self."

"And how do you do that?" Gary asked me. I could see he was already trying to do the math in his head. "That would be great if I could learn how to do that. It would be a lot calmer around here."

"Anyone can learn how to do that," I reassured him. "It's simple, but not easy. I'd like you to think about this morning's situation. Based on the words—your personal values—that you gave me, which of those do you believe was most offended by Evan's behavior?"

"Probably driven," he said. "But maybe fair and honest, also. And passionate and aggressive too, you know. It was like a perfect storm of behaviors . . . there was Evan's behavior, the sales desk manager's behavior, and the customer's behavior all wrapped up in one situation. I thought Evan wasn't driving hard enough, being aggressive enough with the customer, which isn't fair to the dealership, you know. It becomes a lopsided deal. I didn't feel like the customer was being honest, just spouting off a bunch of stuff. And I didn't think the desk manager was passionate enough to want to make the most out of the deal . . . we need to do that with every deal, you know."

"Okay, great. That's a really good analysis, Gary, " I said. "Let's focus on Evan for now. "He did get the brunt of the bang in your flash-bang reaction, right?"

"Yes, he did," he confirmed.

"So in order to diffuse your flash-bang reaction, Gary, what we need to do is eliminate the offensiveness of Evan's behavior. Without the associated offensiveness, the emotion won't be created. If the emotion isn't created, there can't be a reaction; there's no energy for it. Without the reaction, we're left with only a situation . . . a problem to solve."

"Okay, that sounds great. How do we do that?"

"How well do you know Evan?" I asked him.

"I know him well," he said. "He's a great human being. A real stand-up guy."

"Gary, if you had to speculate about how Evan would describe himself to a stranger, how do you think he would do that?"

"I really have no idea about that," he said.

"Well then, how would you describe him based on what you know of him?"

"He's easy going, he's likable, he doesn't rock the boat, he's a sincerely a good guy, he's genuine."

"Do you think he looks for the best in people?"

"That's for sure," he said.

"So, Gary, if Evan were honoring his personal values as you described him, how do you believe he would behave in keeping with those values if working with a customer like he had this morning? Would it be in his nature to suspect that his customer was lying to him, and then challenge that customer to substantiate the claim?"

"No, I don't think it would be," he admitted.

"So, based on the situation this morning, do you believe he was simply honoring his values by behaving the way he did?"

"I suppose he was," he said.

"Now if you can see that Evan was simply honoring his values in his behavior earlier today, is it still as offensive as it was when you thought he was doing it intentionally?"

"No," he said. "I see it completely differently now. It wasn't his fault."

"So, is the emotion gone?" I asked him.

"Yes," he said.

"Okay, great," I applauded. "You've now learned how to interrupt your reactions."

"This is really powerful stuff. You should be on *Dr. Phil* or something."

"I appreciate that," I said. "I'm not sure I'm in Dr. Phil's league just yet, but I really do appreciate you saying that. So again, Gary, you can interrupt your reactions by recognizing that whatever behavior you are witnessing that is offending a personal value of yours is simply someone else behaving with respect to their own values. It really has nothing to do with you whatsoever. They will behave that way whether you're there or not. Their behavior is about them, not you. Your reactions are about you, though, not them. Can you understand how expecting and believing that all others will behave in keeping with your personal values is crazy?"

"I get it," he said.

"Were you proud of the way you treated Evan earlier today?"

"No, of course not."

"Okay then, what's a response you would have been proud of?" I asked.

"Well, I could have coached him," he said. "I could have explained what I was hearing the customer say, how I believed that the customer wasn't being entirely honest with us, that if we didn't challenge his assertions, it would lead to an unfair outcome in his favor. I could have offered to go to talk to the customer myself. I could have supported and helped him," he concluded.

"Perfect," I exclaimed. "That's exactly what I'm talking about. That's how you transform a reaction into a response, turning the interaction from negative to positive, shifting your energy from Conflict to Responsibility. You're willing to take ownership of your own behavior and stop your participation in something called a Super Wicked Problem."

"A super what?" he asked me, laughing.

"A Super Wicked Problem," I repeated. "A Super Wicked Problem exists when those who want to solve the problem, are also causing it. The application here is that you clearly want to level up your interactions with your fellow employees and managers; but at the same time—because you're allowing yourself to be ruled by your emotions as a result of one of your personal values being offended—you have become reactive, and your reactions are destructive, either to yourself or others. When interrupting that reaction, by recognizing that another's behavior is simply them honoring their values, which eliminates the offensiveness associated with the perception of the intentional nature of their behavior, you are able to respond rather than react. You can remain solution oriented and focused on the problem to solve, being a magnitude more effective at both problem solving and interpersonal interactions. And in that way, you have stopped participating in the problem.

The real beauty and power of understanding this is knowing,

if you don't initiate or participate in the Conflict, the Conflict can't exist. The emotion loses its power over you and your behavior. When you allow yourself to be ruled by your emotions, you are really giving your control over to anyone that offends your values; they control your behavior, not you . . . by virtue of your reactions. When you are no longer reactive, you are now fully in charge of yourself. This is a process, Gary. I don't want you to get discouraged. The next time your values get offended, you're going to spin up and flip out . . . same as usual. Then afterward, you'll say to yourself: 'Oh yeah, I wasn't supposed to do that. I was supposed to handle that differently.'

Don't get disappointed," I said again, "it's going to happen. The time after that, you'll interrupt your reaction, mostly by restraint. Meaning that the emotion will still exist, but you'll restrain the most destructive part of the reaction. That will give you some confidence that you don't have to be someone's complete nightmare, 24/7. The time after that though, you'll interrupt your reaction, and the emotional intensity will be dulled. You'll begin to see other's behavior for what it is, them honoring their values. The time after that, the emotion won't exist. You might have even recognized the situation forming, realizing that this particular situation is a 'hot situation,' one prone to offend your values. You'll be ready; you'll begin problem solving.

The situation will be reduced to its lowest common denominator . . . for example: A salesperson is working with a customer, who is attempting to purchase a car at a car dealership somewhere on planet earth. The customer, who isn't trusting of the people or the process at the dealership, has adopted an adversarial posture, employing erroneous details designed to increase their advantage in the buying process. The salesperson, in an effort to preserve the sale and keep the peace, facilitates the purchase by communicating those erroneous details to the sales desk manager and business manager. So in your case, Gary, if we were trying to solve this problem together, would it suggest to you the most effective solution would be to confront, belittle, insult, and embarrass the salesperson, and then throw them out of the Business Office by threat of physical force, in an effort to get them to do the same to their customer, essentially jeopardizing the sale? Would that get us the best outcome?"

"Ah, probably not," he said.

"When you show up to work, Gary, do you say to yourself: My plan today is to be my worst self, and guarantee the worst outcomes?" I asked rhetorically. "No, of course not. Why? Because you need to be your best self. You need to produce the best outcomes, because that's how you'll be most successful. And being most successful at work will allow you to do your best job at providing for your family. Don't show up every day and operate at 50 percent, 60 percent, or even 70 or 80 percent of what your capable of. You're working against yourself in that case. You need to be 95 to 100 percent every day, because that gives you and your family the best life . . . and to get to that next level, it requires leveling up your ability to interact with others. I'm sure our pretend solution sounded crazy to you, but in reality, that was exactly what went on this morning. Reactions do no one any good. I know I sound like I'm preaching now, but the truth is, if you can get this stuff figured out, it will change your life and the lives of the people around you.

RESOLVE: HOW LEARNING TO MANAGE CONFLICT WILL CHANGE YOUR LIFE (AND THE WORLD)

"Resolve, and thou art free."
—Henry Wadsworth Longfellow

It's amazing to me how similar the issues that arise in large organizations are to the issues that arise in our country. The more time I spend working with large companies, the more they come to resemble our nation, and vice-versa. Likewise, the employees of these entities are a small sample of our ever-expanding population, evidencing its incredible strength of diversity, but also revealing its challenges in assimilation.

Take an organization's culture for example. If an organization is culturally strong, when disparate people are added to that culture, those people conform to it. It changes *them*. They adapt to its expectations, its conventions, its policies and procedures, its collective mindset. There is a shared language and a shared experience, a bond, which serves to transform the group—essentially different people who happen to be at the same place, at the same time, with their own individual goals and agendas—into a team. The team is united by common goals and objectives . . . and personal values. Much lip service—and no small fortune—is paid by organizations each year in establishing mission statements, vision statements, and organizational value statements. But it is true that the strongest organizations are welded together by their stated values. Clearly communicating what an organization stands for informs everyone working in that organization what behavior is acceptable, and what isn't. It gives them advanced permission to act in a certain manner. Organizations with crystal-clear values do not need layer upon layer of management to endlessly scrutinize and evaluate every decision made by every employee. They simply educate— inculcate—employees about what the organization stands for, and set the expectation that all employee behavior be a function of that.

Take, for example, one large regional automotive group that I work with. They have established their three-legged stool. The legs of the stool are Customer Satisfaction, Employee Satisfaction, and Profitability, in that order . . . that specific order. Why? Because if one of their employees is faced with solving a customer's issue, and for whatever reason there isn't a manager available to make the decision, that employee can rely on the three legs as a basis for their own decision making. If they resolve the situation by honoring customer satisfaction over profitability, which may result in costing the company some money, that employee should have full confidence that their manager, and their company, will have their back based on them honoring the company's stated values.

The dating website, eHarmony, claims to have the highest percentage of intact relationships of any of its dating website competitors. According to its homepage, its success is driven by its proprietary 29 dimensions of compatibility. As Dr. Neil Clark Warren, the site's founder explains—based on his thirty-five years of counseling couples—he's found that the presence of these dimensions of compatibility within paired couples, becomes indicative of successful long-term relationships. Without knowing the details of the algorithm used by the website, it wouldn't surprise me to learn that the matches are simply based on correlated personal values, essentially matching what's important to those people and the behavior that results. Not too long ago, eHarmony announced on CNBC that it would be launching a division of itself—Elevated Careers—focused on matching prospective employees with potential employers. Again, not knowing anything about the matching methodology at all, it wouldn't surprise me to learn that personal values are at its core. Employees are most rewarded and fulfilled—fully engaged— when they believe that their personal values are represented in the company that they work for and that they are surrounded by like-minded (like-valued) peers.

Conversely, if an organization's values are vaguely communicated, or worse yet, nonexistent, and that organization's culture is weak, when disparate people are added to it, they change *it*. The power structure necessarily transient, with people aligning themselves with whoever they believe has the highest probability of long-term survival, or whoever they feel will help them navigate the rough waters of the organization the most.

Balancing competition with cooperation is another enormous challenge for companies and our country. In a performance-based business, or a performance-based economy, competition is necessary. Capitalism is a meritocracy of sorts. That is, there is a wide distribution of performances and results. It's no different in a business. There are broadly varying instances of success and failure. If a company unknowingly becomes hyper-competitive or ultra-focused on individual results, then its employees will compete with each other; the environment will be marked by an unhealthy dog-eat-dog, every-man-for-himself attitude. Employees will operate in survival mode, and the company will get neither their best, nor the smartest outcomes. If competition is over-valued, a win-at-all-costs mentality will prevail.

Look at Volkswagen Group's recent challenges with respect to their emissions scandal. In a win-or-die culture, employees will do whatever it takes to survive, consequences be damned. Organizations then become siloed, with each employee, department, site, region, market, division, product line, whatever, doing what's best for themselves, while no one is doing what's best for everyone. Competition manifests as an us-against-them mentality in our nation, the haves and the have-nots—the haves feeling fully deserving and entitled, and the have-nots feeling resentful and disadvantaged. If, conversely, companies tilted to fully cooperative, then those companies would suffer from groupthink—alienating anyone with the temerity to challenge the status quo—and be perpetually stuck in a "this is how we've always done it" philosophy. Proper incentives are necessary in a company, or country, to produce the desired behavior. Proving the adage "If you don't get the behavior you want, you don't have the right pay plan," is apt.

Our entire economy is designed around one's own self-interest. Prevailing economic theory states that a rational person acts in a way that seeks to maximize that individual actor's utility. That is, we can expect people to behave in a manner that is good for them, selfishly even. Now, in reality, that may well extend beyond themselves to their family, their companies, any group they identify themselves with, but it's self-serving nonetheless.

This nature in us is what makes problems—like Super Wicked Problems—so intractable. The term Super Wicked Problem was first coined as a phrase to describe global warming. The idea is that we all want to solve global warming, but by our behaviors, even those of us that want to solve the problem also cause it. The incentives to participate in the problem are greater than the payoff related to solving the problem. The imbalance may simply be a function of time. The solution, which might be fifty or one hundred years into the future, may not provide enough utility to the rational actors to change their behavior today. The benefactors, that is the generations of the future, have no ability to appeal to or impact the behavior of those in the present. Someone concerned about surviving today has no interest in a future benefit for their heirs, or for themselves for that matter. Their immediate survival precludes their long-term thoughts.

But a Super Wicked Problem has a weakness, and it is disguised as a strength. Much like the virologist, Dr. Andrew Fassbach, in the movie *World War Z* explained, "Mother Nature is a serial killer. No one's better or more creative. Like all serial killers, she can't help the urge to want to get caught. What good are all those brilliant crimes if no one takes the credit? So she leaves crumbs. Now the hard part, why you spend a decade in school, is seeing the crumbs. But the clue's there. Sometimes the thing you thought was the most brutal aspect of the virus, turns out to be the chink in its armor. And she loves disguising her weaknesses as strengths. She's a bitch."

The Super Wicked Problem's weakness is in its reliance on the inability of participants to stop participating in it. Much of that participation is driven by emotion and reaction. Just listen to any debate about global warming. It won't be a civil dialogue about which solution is most likely to solve it. It will be a passion brawl, with opposition on each side debating whether the problem even exists. It will focus on the cost, or more precisely who's going to pay the cost, the inequity of the regulations with respect to any of the developing nation's handicapped by those regulations. Each party defending their position, likely to the death if necessary. The topic of global warming itself, along with its perceived winners and losers, could certainly spark armed conflict at any moment. Abortion, the death penalty, gay rights, religion, politics, it's no different. The conversations had are marked by such heightened emotions—polarizing emotions, the hallmark of a Super Wicked Problem's survival strategy—that a rational conversation is impossible. The focus instead is on forwarding a career, countering an argument, advancing an agenda, all the while making the problem itself unsolvable.

But with respect to Conflict, the Super Wicked Problem has met its match. Why, you ask? Because in the case of managing Conflict, the incentives are exactly right to produce the individual and collective behavior to defeat the Super Wicked Problem, rendering it more a tiny distraction or nuisance. In order to manage Conflict, one must stop participating in the Conflict. By not participating in the Conflict, one is more often their best self, producing smarter outcomes and enjoying a more peaceful existence. I can't imagine anyone opting for an interaction with the old me, versus the new me. That would be dangerous and dumb. So, opting to stop participating in the Conflict *is* behaving in keeping with maximizing one's utility. It *is* in one's best interest to not participate in the Conflict. The incentive to stop participating *is greater* than the incentive to perpetuate it. As a result, Conflict will be greatly reduced for that individual and all individuals that that person interacts with. Likewise, for anyone else who learns how to stop participating. If enough people stop participating, Conflict will become an endangered species. And situations will be more often seen for what they truly are . . . just problems to be solved.

As I was finishing this book, there were a series of deadly attacks carried out by ISIS in Paris, France. The attacks killed 128 people and injured many, many, more. Following those attacks, days later, in Mali, a hostage situation ended with more than a dozen dead as well. As a result of those attacks, there has been no end to the analysis on the local, network, and cable news channels. The analyses often including references to our country's values. Our values as a nation and as a people, but also more broadly, in the sense of universal values, of *all* people. The tones are mostly reactive and focused on *defending* our values. What we need to do offensively, to hunt down and capture or kill the threat. To once and for all eradicate the truly unthinkable behavior by any force necessary. Of course, these reactions are normal, and natural. People have been murdered, the ultimate offense with respect to valuing human life. It's also the ultimate victimization, ending one's existence due to an uncontrollable circumstance. Helplessness, powerlessness, hopelessness, despair, despondency, and inevitability prevail. Rebelling against that with all one's might, and summoning the vast strength and capabilities of the world's armies—assembled, focused, and propelled by the sheer effrontery, and inhumanity, of the offender's inconceivable actions—is altogether prudent and completely practical. But, at the same time, in an incredibly unfair, impossibly counterintuitive, and tragically ironic way, we will also be actively creating the behavior in our aggressors that we don't want.

The simple fact is that force met with force perpetuates conflict. I've spent most of my life meeting everything with force—force with force, and not-force with force—meeting conflict, when it existed, and creating it, when it didn't. The outcomes were mixed. I either lost the confrontation, or created a loser by virtue of my winning the confrontation at the other's expense. At the same time, I spawned resentment; temporarily restrained or hidden hostility, assiduous and patient saboteurs, and willing co-conspirators. What I never got though, was the *smartest* outcome. The smartest outcome is produced when one's energies and brainpower are keenly focused on solving a problem. And the most unfortunate and devastating reality of reacting in a situation is that the problem remains. It persists; it outlives, out maneuvers, and outthinks its passionate conquerors. Its sole defense, dependent on emotions stifling thought. Rendering all reactions ineffectual, like trying to solve a Rubik's Cube with a hammer.

I don't have a PhD in anything. I'm not a master or guru of an esoteric, or obscure, method. I don't meditate to connect to the collective unconscious, or follow the teachings of any spiritual guides. I just understand Conflict on a deep level. I understand it, because I lived it; I *was* it. It took me forty-six years to learn that I was the source of the Conflict in my own life; that I was part of a Super Wicked Problem—wanting to solve the problem while also causing it, being ruled by my emotions, seldom my best self, scarcely producing the best outcomes and never the smartest ones.

And it has to be about producing the smartest outcomes. In a world with over 7 billion people, 196 countries, 7000 languages spoken, close to 30 different religions with more than 1 million members; the probability of one group intentionally or unintentionally offending the values of another group, or one person intentionally or unintentionally offending the values of another person is absolutely certain. It's a one, on a probability scale of zero to one. It is a given that one's personal values will be offended. There will be certain situations that are prone for that to happen, depending on the person or group involved. The party offended will become emotional, providing them the energy necessary for action or, in the case of Conflict, reaction. The emotional energy is created in them because they do not want the situation to be as it is; they want it to be different in some way. They're not able to fathom a world, where the situation as it currently exists, is a place they would want to be. It's inscrutable to them. For them, it is an absolute must that the offending behavior be changed. Simultaneously, they will be perfectly blinded to their own participation in the situation, reserving any measure of contempt or shame for full reassignment to the supposed offender—judged by an impossibly biased and myopic perspective, straight from a world view with a population of one.

In that exact moment, we either continue the chain of reactions or we remain pure in thought, solution oriented, welcoming the smartest outcome. That is achieved by acknowledging that *all* human behavior is a function of personal values, and recognizing that conflict exists when someone feels like one of their personal values has been offended or when someone feels like another is imposing their personal values on them. Owning the fact that we sometimes create the behavior in others that we don't want. Learning about the specific situations that are prone to offend our personal values, in order to anticipate them, manage them, and proactively avoid them. Admitting that, when one of our personal values is offended, we become emotionally charged, armed and ready for action, or more appropriately described, reaction. When we are reactive, we are not our best selves, nor do we produce the best outcomes, we are unable to think rationally, due to the thought-stopping nature of an emotional hijacking. We create winners and losers, in either ourselves or others, based on our default style of reaction. Unable to see others' behavior as them honoring their values, the keystone to eliminating the offensiveness perceived by that behavior, and then transforming the reaction into a response, flipping it from a negative interaction to a positive one. Not only eliminating conflict from that interaction, but eliminating conflict altogether from every interaction.

There are vast resources of available brainpower on this planet. The XPRIZE, for example, harnesses the thoughts and energies of contestants competing with each other to solve some of the world's greatest challenges. The Nobel Prize goes about that too, similarly. I'd love to see a new world body, with our primary conflicts as topics, as well. Let's try to solve capitalism versus communism, Islamic fundamentalism versus the Western religions, rich versus poor, white versus Black and Hispanic and Asian, too, but rationally, not emotionally. As our best selves, seeking only the smartest outcomes.

When I'm working directly with people struggling with conflict, I often ask them to offer me some suggestions to the problems they're struggling with, packaged differently, presented to them as the problems of others elsewhere. It allows them to dispassionately look at the problem, remaining solution oriented and pure of thought. If I were to do that with some of the situations we face today as a society, I might set it up this way: Let's fast-forward one thousand years. I'm now a Planetary Coach. I've been hired by a planet's Leadership Team to help them work through some of the issues they face in their growing civilization.

"Hey folks," I might begin. "I need your help today. I'm working with another planet in the galaxy. On this planet, they are struggling with different peoples, who inhabit different parts of the planet, speak different languages, follow different religious conventions, are members of different nations, with different ideologies, different economic structures, and who are willing to kill each other to advance their own beliefs. What are some things you might suggest that I could take back to that Planetary Leadership Team to help them get that figured out?"

After some super serious consideration, I bet the top suggestion would not be to have each constituent group build the strongest army possible; locate and target all members of opposing constituent groups, beginning with the group's furthest away with respect to one's agreement of thought; and, if unable to sufficiently neutralize the threat locally, use weapons of mass destruction to destroy the largest number of them, fastest. Why? Because after all the bodies are buried, the fires are put out, the buildings are reconstructed, the accords are signed, and the economies restored, the problems will remain unsolved. Just with fewer people left to fight the next time.

Now, I could imagine that being a suggestion during an impassioned argument, while people were polarized emotionally and reacting in Conflict. But, when it's not about them, but somewhere else, with someone else, they aren't emotionally invested. And that's why I position it the way I do:

"I need your help today. I'm working with another planet in the galaxy. On this planet, they are struggling with different peoples who inhabit different parts of the planet, speak different languages, follow different religious conventions, are members of different nations, with different ideologies, different economic structures, and who are willing to kill each other to advance their own beliefs."

So, now it's your turn . . . what are some things *you* might suggest that I could take back to that Planetary Leadership Team to help them get that figured out?"

AFTERWORD

O n May 11th, 2016 I received an email from my father's sister. As always, she began her note asking about my son, and then proceeded to tell me that she had been contacted by a woman from Scotland who believed she was my half-sister. I must say I had to read the email a number of times to let the news sink in. My aunt's email said that the woman shared that her mother had been married to my father, and that they lived south of Indianapolis somewhere. The woman also shared a memory of my father's mother making dresses for her when the woman was an infant. My aunt said that the woman had expressed an interest in contacting me, but my aunt would not provide her my contact information without my prior approval. Instead she forwarded me the woman's contact information, and said that she felt the woman "needed to find her family."

I let the news settle for a few hours, unsure about how I would respond. Later that evening, I wrote a note to the woman. I shared that I had contacted my aunt as well back in 1992, which ultimately led to me meeting my father. I explained that, initially, he and I had a relationship, but I hadn't talked to him since 2003. I shared that I was surprised by the message, but not the circumstance. After all, I had lived it myself (see below):

> *Late this afternoon I received an email from my (our) aunt. I must say the message surprised me, but the circumstance did not.*
>
> *In 1992, I contacted her as well . . . searching for my father. My parents separated when I was a year old. I met my father for the first time when I was 27.*
>
> *I wish I could say the story had a happy ending. He did try in the beginning, but over time it was obvious he didn't want much to do with me, or his grandson. I haven't talked to him since 2003.*
>
> *He also has another child. We never connected.*
>
> *I turned 51 this past February. The picture below was taken for my passport.*
>
> *I'd be happy to talk if you'd like.*

I remember worrying about the lack of sensitivity in the message, but I didn't want to paint a happy picture . . . it wasn't one.

On May 14th, 2016, the woman wrote me back. She explained that her mother and my father were never married. She said that she had often been described as "illegitimate" as a child. That admission was heartbreaking for me to read. At the very least, my membership to the family was never challenged. I was the fourth Richard, my middle name was after my father's uncle, the OB/GYN that delivered me at Indiana University Medical Center. I was the first born, and the only son. My mother was my father's first wife.

The thought of someone's being thought of as illegitimate brought tears to my eyes and re-sparked the rage in me that existed for most of my life.

I thought about my father not only abandoning one child, but now two. TWO! The first time may have been a mistake, and as a young, immature parent, I can imagine him feeling trapped and wanting to escape. But a second time?! Once is unforgivable . . . twice? There are no words sufficient to capture that.

When she shared her age, the dots started to connect. She said she would be forty-nine this year, in July. That meant she was born in 1967, and a month earlier than my wife. Then I did the math back to conception, roughly in October of 1966. I spent my first birthday in Indianapolis: February 1966. After that it gets fuzzy. My mother took me back to Rhode Island at some point after my first birthday and before my second. Within eight months of my first birthday, this woman was conceived. Given how she described remembering living with her mother and my father in Liverpool, England, when she was around two (1969), it seems a fair assumption that there was some relationship that preceded and followed the birth. The timing could mean that the affair between my father and her mother was exactly the event that caused my mother to leave him and take me back to Rhode Island.

Unfortunately, I can't ask my mother about the development . . . she died in 2001. My aunt said my father "wasn't forthcoming with information" about the circumstance. No surprise really. He just decides that there are things he's not willing to remember for his own preservation's sake, then for him they never happened. Life must be easy without the kind of accountability that most other human beings subject themselves to. I imagine behavior of any kind must be okay with him then, given that he simply decides that he doesn't have to deal with any of the aftermath, ever.

In her note to me, the woman expressed her disbelief of no one in the family searching for her. I understood that. No one searched for me either. She said that she had learned to cope with the situation as she got older, but that she wasn't sure she could have handled the "harshness of the reality" when she was younger. I know I couldn't deal with it then; I can barely deal with it now. But unlike me, she didn't punish herself and everyone around her for most of her life. For her, rage was quiet.

In the military, I learned that hardships forge human beings together for life. It's the shared life experiences that create lifelong kinships that previously hadn't existed, and probably never would have. Me and the woman who contacted me share a life experience that no two other people on the planet share; we were both abandoned by the same man.

In the weeks that followed her initial contact, she and my wife exchanged numerous emails, along with small tokens of friendship. Ours from UCLA, where my son is currently a student, and hers from Inverness, Scotland. At some point, we'll begin to piece together the details that occurred over fifty years ago, our shared details, those that ultimately led to the writing of this book.

APPENDIX

— Operating Philosophy —

* Life is Hard
* People Suck
* Things Can't Change   } Life
* I Can't Break Through   } Sentence
* I'm Not Good Enough

— Behaviors —

* Expect The Worst in People
* Slow To Trust
* Prefer to Compete, Rather Than Cooperate
* Eternally on Guard
* Suspect A hidden Agenda
* Do what's Best for yourself.

Take a moment to think about the operational imperatives that you believe exist in your world. What are they? Make a list. List as many as you can. Next, explain in behavioral terms how your behavior is in keeping with those beliefs. Are they healthy and positive, or are they limiting and negative? Are they serving you, or are you serving them? Does it describe a world that you want to live in? How would you like your world to be different? What are you doing about it?

How Conflict is Negatively Impacting My Life:

* FEEL LIKE I'm IN ONE ENDLESS ARGUMENT
* THANKLESS JOB
* Thankless Life
* Broken Relationships
* SUCCESS @ THE EXPENSE of OTHERS
* loss of Job, Income
* loss of professional Confidence
* UNSURE ABOUT The ABility to Continuously Provide for my family
* WIFE AND SON AFRAID of ME

*** Periodically throughout the book, I'll ask you to complete certain exercises. The first of which is to conduct a self-assessment, much the way I did, to understand how conflict is negatively impacting your life. Grab a pen and a tablet, take a few minutes, and make a list for yourself. Be brutally honest. Change is a function of increased self-awareness and awareness of others. This is the first step toward that increased self-awareness.***

Declaring Personal Values

Pretend you are describing yourself to a
stranger, and you want that stranger
to know everything about you, that
you'd want them to know, in six, eight,
or ten words. What are those words?

VALUES

* Successful
* Passionate
* TrustWorthy
* Hand-Working
* Generous

* Selfless
* Competitive
* Caring
* Thoughtful
* Positive

*** Please take a moment, grab a pen and a tablet, and think about the request. Pretend you are describing yourself to a stranger, and you'd like that stranger to know everything about you that you'd want them to know in six, or eight, or ten words. What are those words?***

Hot Situations

- Tell me about a Situation that tends to bring out your worst... That turns you into that person that you don't want to be, but are anyway.

- If multiple Situations, Try to identify the most frequent, or most intense?

- Take the time to be back in the moment, hear the sounds, smell the smells — Try to be fully present.

Situations:

Marty —

That's easy... It's when I'm alone, on the phone, the guy I work with is off another, an two guys at the counter.

Take a moment. Grab a pen and a tablet. Think about the request: "Tell me about a situation that tends to bring out your worst, that turns you into that person that you don't want to be but are anyway." If there are multiple situations, try to identify the most frequent or the most intense. Take the time to be back in the moment, try to hear the sounds, and smell the smells. Try to be fully present in that moment.

ABOUT THE AUTHOR

I never imagined I would think these thoughts, feel these feelings, or write these words, but I find myself thankful and indebted to the circumstances and the rage. That combination powered me through my life. Without which, I could not be who I am today. After all these many years, I have been blessed and am grateful to have finally engaged and conquered the source of my conflict. And by knowing conflict, I am now able to truly value and enjoy peace.

I would love to hear about your personal experience with conflict. Feel free to share your experience, comments, or questions: rwburke@coachingconflict.com

Author photo © Richard Burke

SELECTED TITLES FROM SPARKPRESS

SparkPress is an independent boutique publisher delivering high-quality, entertaining, and engaging content that enhances readers' lives, with a special focus on female-driven work. Visit us at www.gosparkpress.com

The Natives are Restless, Constance Hale. $40, 978-1-943006-06-9. Journalist Constance Hale presents the largely untold story of the dance tradition of hula, using the twin keyholes of Kumu Patrick Makuakane (a Hawaii-born, San Francisco-based hula master), and his 350-person arts organization. In the background, she weaves the poignant story of an ancient people and the resilience of their culture.

The House that Made Me: Writers Reflect on the Places and People That Defined Them, edited by Grant Jarret. $17, 978-1-940716-31-2. In this candid, evocative collection of essays, a diverse group of acclaimed authors reflect on the diverse homes, neighborhoods, and experiences that helped shape them—using Google Earth software to revisit the location in the process.

Gravel on the Side of The Road: True Stories From a Broad Who Has Been There, Kris Radish. $15, 978-1-940716-43-5. A woman who worries about carrying a .38 special in he rpurse, nearly drowns in a desert canyon, flies into the war in Bosnia, dances with the FBI, and spends time with murderers, has more than a few stories to tell. This daring and revealing adventured by beloved novelist Kris Radish is her first book of autobiographical essays.

Potty-Mouthed: Big Thoughts for Little Brains, $19.95, 978-1-943006-30-4. An illustrated collection of the hilarious things kids say, collected by a couple as they stagger through the punch-in-the-gut and laugh-out-loud moments all parents experience while raising new talkers.

Funny Little Pregnant Things: The good, the bad, and the just plain gross things about pregnancy that other books aren't going to tell you, Emily Doherty, $17, 978-1-940716-58-9. For all the women out there who aren't interested in boring run of the mill pregnancy advice, a book that tells the real—and hilarious—truth about the good, bad, and sometimes ugly stuff that comes before, during, and after pregnancy.

ABOUT SPARKPRESS

SparkPress is an independent, hybrid imprint focused on merging the best of the traditional publishing model with new and innovative strategies. We deliver high-quality, entertaining, and engaging content that enhances readers' lives. We are proud to bring to market a list of *New York Times* best-selling, award-winning, and debut authors who represent a wide array of genres, as well as our established, industry-wide reputation for creative, results-driven success in working with authors. SparkPress, a BookSparks imprint, is a division of SparkPoint Studio LLC.

Learn more at GoSparkPress.com

CPSIA information can be obtained
at www.ICGtesting.com
Printed in the USA
BVOW06*1026150917

494824BV00007B/28/P